YORK NOTE

General Editors: Professor A.N. J
of Stirling) & Professor Suheil Bu
University of Beirut)

T. S. Eliot

THE COCKTAIL PARTY

Notes by Dominic Hyland

MA (CAMBRIDGE) M ED (MANCHESTER)
Tutor-Counsellor with the Open University

LONGMAN
YORK PRESS

YORK PRESS
Immeuble Esseily, Place Riad Solh, Beirut.

LONGMAN GROUP LIMITED
Longman House,
Burnt Mill,
Harlow,
Essex.

First published 1985
ISBN 0 582 79245 2
Printed in Hong Kong by
Sheck Wah Tong Printing Press Ltd

Contents

Part 1

Introduction

The life of T. S. Eliot

Thomas Stearns Eliot was born on 26 September 1888, the seventh and youngest child of Henry Ware Eliot and Charlotte Stearns. He was born in St Louis, a large industrial city in Missouri in the United States of America. Eliot could trace his ancestry back to Andrew Eliot, an Englishman who left East Coker in Somerset in 1670 and settled in Massachusetts in the United States. Another ancestor, the Reverend William Greenleaf Eliot, established the first Unitarian church and founded Washington University. Eliot thus belonged to a family with a rich religious and academic background.

His early education was at Smith Academy in St Louis. We are told that he learned to love and admire English Victorian poetry. The poem that he claimed changed his life was the world-famous translation of *The Rubaiyat of Omar Khayyam* by the English poet Edward Fitzgerald (1809–83). At the age of sixteen Eliot made some contributions in prose and poetry to the *Smith Academy Record*.

In 1905, at the age of seventeen, Eliot spent a year at Milton Academy in Massachusetts, and then entered Harvard University in 1906 and remained there until 1914. The philosopher and critic George Santayana (1863–1952) taught a course at that time at Harvard called 'History of Modern Philosophy', and this led Eliot to interest himself in philosophy. Following this interest he engaged in an intensive study of philosophy after graduation, during the years 1911–15. At Harvard he also met Irving Babbitt (1865–1933), the eminent literary critic who taught an M.A. course called 'Literary Criticism in France with Special Reference to the Nineteenth Century'. One book that Eliot claimed had an immediate effect on his perception of literature at this time was *The Symbolist Movement in Literature* (1899) by Arthur Symons (1865–1945), the British poet and critic.

In 1910 Eliot went to Paris to spend a year working at the Sorbonne. In 1911, he returned to Harvard where he commenced his studies for a doctorate. The subject of his dissertation was the work of the British philosopher F. H. Bradley (1846–1924). Bradley was interested in the conflict between appearance and reality, and in his work *Appearance and Reality* (1893) he claimed that we were concerned more with the appearance of things than with their reality. The British philosopher Bertrand

Russell (1872–1970) met Eliot at this time and spoke highly of him. He clearly possessed a charisma: many people who met Eliot both then and later were struck by his good looks.

In 1914 Eliot went to London where he met the American poet Ezra Pound (1885–1972). Pound admired Eliot's poetry and did his utmost to persuade Harold Munro, the owner of the Poetry Bookshop and editor of *Poetry and Drama*, to publish Eliot's poems. Munro refused, but Pound continued to show considerable enthusiasm for Eliot's work and particularly for the poem 'The Love Song of J. Alfred Prufrock' which first appeared in June 1915 in the magazine *Poetry*.

In October 1914 Eliot went to Merton College, Oxford, for his last year as a philosophy student. There he completed his doctoral dissertation and despatched it to Harvard. It had considerable merit but Eliot never received his doctorate for he never returned to the United States. In 1927 he was to renounce his American citizenship and become a British subject.

The year following his arrival in England, Eliot married his first wife Vivien Haigh Haigh-Wood, the daughter of an English painter. It did not prove a happy marriage. In his autobiography, Bertrand Russell has this to say of the early days of this relationship:

> He is exquisite and listless; she says she married him to stimulate him, he finds she can't do it. Obviously, he married in order to be stimulated. I think she will soon be tired of him . . . . He is ashamed of his marriage and very grateful if one is kind to her.*

Bertrand Russell was very generous to the Eliots – he lent them a room in his flat, and gave T. S. Eliot three hundred pounds' worth of engineering debentures (interest-earning securities issued by a company in return for a loan of money). In 1918, he lent them a house at Marlow in Buckinghamshire. Many of Eliot's friends were similarly concerned about the relationship between him and his wife. She was an hysteric, and suffered from frequent bouts of depression and mental illness. They separated in 1933, and Vivien died in 1947.

In 1915 Eliot took up teaching, first at High Wycombe Grammar School, and then at Highgate Junior School in north London. One of his pupils there was the poet John Betjeman (*b*.1906) who (at the age of ten!) presented him with a book of his own poetry entitled *The Best of Betjeman*. Teaching did not appeal to Eliot and he took up a career in banking instead, joining Lloyds Bank in London. He rose to a post of some importance in that institution and was highly regarded. He was a very capable executive and it was because of his abilities in this field that he was offered a position with a publishing firm, Faber and Gwyer, in

The Autobiography of Bertrand Russell, George Allen and Unwin, London, 1968, Vol. II, p. 54.

1925. He later became a director of this firm when it became Faber and Faber.

The years between 1917 and 1925 were busy years for Eliot as a man of letters. In 1917 he published his first collection of poems, which took its title from the first poem in the volume, 'The Love Song of J. Alfred Prufrock'. Other poems in the collection were the 'Preludes', the 'Portrait of a Lady', and 'Rhapsody on a Windy Night'. All these poems had first appeared in 1915 in various poetry magazines. Between 1917 and 1919 he was the literary editor for the magazine *The Egoist*, and he founded the magazine *The Criterion* in 1922. In that same year one of his best-known poems *The Waste Land* appeared in the magazine *The Dial* and won that magazine's annual award of two thousand dollars. In December of that year it was published in book form by Boni and Liveright, New York.

Eliot's literary output was not limited to poetry, and the years following his appointment to Faber and Gwyer saw the appearance of many of his critical essays. It was in one of his works of criticism, *The Use of Poetry* (1933), that he expressed his opinion that the theatre was the ideal medium for poetry. Eliot's first attempt at drama was a pageant play called *The Rock* (1933), produced at the Sadler's Wells Theatre, London, from 28 May to 9 June 1934. This was followed by a commercially more successful play, *Murder in the Cathedral* (1935), first performed in Canterbury Cathedral and then at two theatres in London, the Mercury and the Duchess.

These two plays had religious messages of a Christian nature. Eliot had been confirmed in the Church of England in 1927 and was a convinced Christian. In this he was often at odds with the intellectual climate of the time which was generally agnostic if not atheistic. The horrors of the First World War had led to a conviction that God was dead and faith was meaningless. Eliot's own lack of optimism about the world and its meaning had found expression in his poem *The Waste Land*. Yet, despite all this, Eliot embraced orthodox Christianity. Evil, according to Christian belief, can be attributed to the existence of sin in the world, and the theme of the necessity for doing penance for sin, the need to suffer because of evil, is central to his next play, *The Family Reunion* (1939). There are some echoes of the same theme in *The Cocktail Party*, written ten years later, in 1949, but it is a far lighter and dramatically more successful play than *The Family Reunion*.

Before the success of *The Cocktail Party* in 1949 Eliot was awarded in December 1948 the Nobel Prize for Literature and, earlier in the same year, the high honour of the Order of Merit. Eliot had suddenly become a public figure – it is recorded that he lectured in the University of Minnesota to nearly fifteen thousand people on 'The Frontiers of Criticism'.

His next play, *The Confidential Clerk*, was performed in 1953 and was also well received. This was in contrast to his last play, *The Elder Statesman* (1958) which has been seen as mirroring to some extent his private life, and his marriage in 1957 to his secretary, Valerie Fletcher. His second marriage appears to have brought him happiness which lasted to his death. He died after a long illness on 4 January 1965.

Literary background

Arthur Symons's book *The Symbolist Movement in Literature* (1899) exercised a considerable influence on T. S. Eliot's view of poetry. The work of the Symbolist poets, most of whom were French, stood in contrast to that of the Realist school. The latter had a direct social aim, to bring about a change in society, and there was a reforming zeal about it. The Symbolists did not see the role of the poet in this way. They concentrated on poetry for its own sake, showing a concern for forms and expression. They have often been accused of deliberate obscurity and superficial erudition. Certainly their work is full of allusions to literature and other fields, and dwells largely on the intangible workings of the mind. The two French Symbolist poets who most influenced Eliot were Charles Baudelaire (1821–67) and Jules Laforgue (1860–87). In an essay on the former, Eliot has this to say:

> It is not merely in the use of imagery of common life, not merely in the use of imagery of the sordid life of a great metropolis, but in the eleva-tion of such imagery to the *first intensity* – presenting it as it is, and yet making it represent something much more than itself – that Baudelaire has created a mode of release and expression for other men.*

Eliot did not praise innovation for innovation's sake. He was a great traditionalist and saw one of the poet's roles as to strive to use the best of literary tradition and restore neglected features of great traditions of the past. At the same time, he saw it as essential that the poet should recognise and not ignore the impulse of the times in which he lived.

It was his great awareness of the great literary English tradition that led Eliot to show the relevance of such great poets as John Donne (1572–1631), the Metaphysical poet, and his contemporaries to the twentieth century. While he was willing to speak of these contemporaries as 'The School of Donne' Eliot resisted the notion that he himself belonged to any such modern 'school'. It is true that through his friend Ezra Pound he was closely linked with a group calling themselves the Imagists who based their attitudes towards poetry on Baudelaire's. He would have

*Selected Essays, Faber and Faber, London, 1932, p. 426.

resisted being labelled as an Imagist though much of his poetry displays all of the six so-called aims of the Imagists, namely, 'precision, new rhythms, free subject, presenting an image, hard clarity, and concentration'.

Eliot's attitude towards poetry and tradition is well reflected in his theory of poetic drama. He claimed that people had come to think of prose as being the natural medium for dramatic expression and saw verse as restrictive. Critics of poetry in drama, says Eliot, claim that

> People were once content with a restricted and artificial range of emotion. Only prose can give the full gamut of modern feeling, can correspond to actuality. But is not every dramatic representation artificial? And are we not merely deceiving ourselves when we aim at greater and greater realism? Are we not contenting ourselves with appearances instead of insisting on fundamentals . . . I say that prose drama is merely a slight by-product of verse drama. The human soul in intense emotion strives to express itself in verse . . . . The tendency, at any rate, of prose drama is to emphasise the ephemeral and superficial; if we want to get to the permanent and universal we tend to express ourselves in verse.*

In his concern for reality as against mere appearance Eliot hearkens back to his philosophical training and, in particular, to his study of the British philosopher F. H. Bradley. But Eliot was not merely a theoriser. He was not one of those poets who had no knowledge of the stage. He studied dramatic technique at first hand and would rewrite his plays depending on the way in which the players could or could not handle his work. He saw that his plays must not be merely 'poetry shaped into a dramatic form'.†

Twentieth-century drama in England was greatly influenced by European writers. Bertolt Brecht (1898–1956), the German dramatist, saw the theatre as a medium for social comment, and we see evidence of his influence in the so-called 'kitchen sink' plays of the 1950s and 1960s in England. August Strindberg (1849–1912), the Swedish playwright, was influential in the expressionist drama in England in which the dramatist builds his play round the expression of a state of mind. Eugene Ionesco (b.1912) is another exponent of this type of drama in which action is largely absent since the main thrust is the expression of a mood or a state of mind. A third form of drama popular at this time was that of the so-called 'well-made play' (where the main intention is not didactic or philosophical but dramatic). Writers of such plays feel a need to produce a play that will appeal to the ordinary theatre-goer. The ingredients will be those of interesting and varied characters, a plot that compels interest,

---

*Selected Essays, Faber and Faber, London, 1932, p. 46.
†Poetry and Drama, Faber and Faber, London, 1951, p. 12.

plenty of action, and familiar, recognisable settings. It is into this third category, that of the 'well-made play', that *The Cocktail Party* most easily fits. It does not, however, exclude themes or intentions that were always close to Eliot's mind.

Such didactic intentions are muted, certainly by comparison with, say, Eliot's earlier play, *Murder in the Cathedral* (1935). In that play, too, Eliot's verse had been more obtrusive, whereas in *The Cocktail Party* he uses a blank verse form that, according to one critic, 'seems to serve only as a kind of notation to assist the actors'.* The same critic goes on to say that 'Eliot's decisive mistake was undoubtedly to exaggerate the centrality and potentialities of the rather tired mode of naturalistic theatre that he at length adopted, after spurning it for so long. The irony is that he did so just before the advent of Beckett† as a dramatist and the delayed impact of Brecht in the English theatre showed the immense possibilities of an expressive and non-naturalistic drama, even without the obligation of being formally poetic.'‡

In contrast to the truly revolutionary effects of the plays of a dramatist such as Samuel Beckett, Eliot's own early promise of bringing about a reform in English theatre was never fully realised. Speaking of this, Sean Lucy has written:

At times, he seems to desire a real reform in the drama, a radical transformation of the theatre, but generally his aim seems limited to trying to make verse drama acceptable in the realist theatre. All the same, it is possible to reconcile the two aims if one considers that a real reform can be effected by gradual change just as efficiently as by revolution. Eliot's attempt to win over the enemy citadel by peaceful penetration – to reform rather than flatly oppose – is a typically traditional measure.§

A note on the text

Eliot was a careful reviser of his plays and was prepared to change his script according to the experience of the actors who performed it. His first producer, E. Martin Browne, tells us that 'He was always a meticulous worker, hence a fairly slow one.'** In the same essay on Eliot, Browne gives an account of the play's development.

On 18 July, 1948, he sent me the first draft of three acts; and on the title page was the name *One-Eyed Riley*. But the alternative title was

*Bernard Bergonzi, *T. S. Eliot*, The Macmillan Company, New York, 1972, p. 187.
†Samuel Beckett (*b.*1906), Irish dramatist who settled in France in 1932. His plays ignore many of the conventions of theatre.
‡Bergonzi, *op.cit.*, p. 187.
§Sean Lucy, *T. S. Eliot and the Idea of Tradition*, Cohen and West, London, 1960, p. 182.
**'T. S. Eliot in the Theatre' in *T. S. Eliot, The Man and his Work*, ed. Allen Tate, Chatto and Windus, London, 1967, p. 130.

already in discussion, and soon *The Cocktail Party* was agreed upon . . . . This draft is a fascinating document; as one compares it with the final script, one can see the process by which the style of the post-war comedies developed. In the draft there are a good number of cryptic observations. In the final version, these are almost eliminated in favour of direct statement. The verse likewise is shorn of imagery and evocative phrases, and the repetitions . . . are made to appear natural. In form, too, there is a steady development towards comedy and towards a natural flow.

The draft contains all the chief scenes of what are now Acts I and II.*

Early in 1949, Browne goes on to relate, he took 'the three quarters of the play which I had in first draft. The joints had not yet been made between the scenes, and there was no last act'.† In the original last act that was written in time for the play's performance at the Edinburgh Festival in Summer 1949 Celia's crucifixion was made a very real thing! However, there was protest at this and Eliot toned it down a great deal. Browne tells us that 'no dramatist was ever more willing to attend to critical questions and suggestions, especially from the one who had to make the play work on stage'.‡

These Notes are based upon the paperback edition of T. S. Eliot, *The Cocktail Party*, Faber and Faber, London, 1958.

*Browne, *op. cit.*, pp. 127–8.
†*Ibid.*, p. 129.
‡*Ibid.*, p. 130.

Part 2

Summaries
of THE COCKTAIL PARTY

A general summary

The play opens in the drawing-room of a London flat owned by Edward and Lavinia Chamberlayne. When the play begins, we find that these two are husband and wife, but at this moment are at odds with one another and are separated. Neither of them is blameless, for Edward Chamberlayne, a lawyer, has a mistress called Celia Coplestone, and Lavinia is in love with a young man called Peter Quilpe. Both Quilpe and Celia Coplestone are writers – he is a film-script writer, she a poet. An added complication is that Peter Quilpe is in love with Celia Coplestone.

The play opens with a cocktail party. Lavinia is not present and Edward makes the excuse that she is away visiting a sick aunt. In addition to the characters already mentioned there are three other guests at the party. One is a friend called Julia Shuttlethwaite who, we discover, is avid for any hint of scandal, and another is a man called Alexander MacColgie Gibbs, who has travelled extensively and has connections with the Foreign Office. The third guest is described as 'an Unidentified Guest'. He later proves to be Sir Henry Harcourt-Reilly, a consultant psychiatrist, and in Act II of the play we find Edward, Lavinia and Celia all consulting him professionally. Acting jointly with him in treating these three people are Alexander MacColgie Gibbs and Julia.

Through Sir Henry's advice Edward and Lavinia are reconciled. Celia, with Sir Henry's encouragement, seeks her own salvation. We later learn that she joined a medical missionary order and lost her life in a gruesome and tragic manner. The news of her death is given by Alex in Act III at another cocktail party at which Sir Henry Harcourt-Reilly is again present. Alex and Julia and Sir Henry are the three 'Guardians' in the play, and it seems to be their function to help to guide the other characters to their destinies.

Detailed summaries

Act I	Scene 1

The play opens with a cocktail party being held in the London flat of Edward Chamberlayne, a lawyer. The cocktail party, we learn later in this scene, is a mistake. It had been arranged by Chamberlayne's wife but she had subsequently left him! He tried to cancel the party but did not know how to contact some of the guests. The result was that four of these had arrived in addition to one man whom we only know in this scene as the Unidentified Guest. Edward never really insists on learning his name, and he never volunteers it.

The party opens in light-hearted mood with some banter between two of the guests, Alexander MacColgie Gibbs and Julia Shuttlethwaite. He had been telling a story which she had not fully understood, and he refuses to repeat any details. The other guests then encourage Julia herself to tell a story which they already know well, but which she tells with some style. The story is about 'Lady Klootz and the wedding cake.' We are never to find out any details about this story other than the single fact that Lady Klootz was discovered by the butler, rinsing out her mouth with champagne. Julia herself sees the story as an opportunity to recite a kind of *Who's Who* of their social circle, and we learn that the Unidentified Guest is unfamiliar with every name that she mentions. There are some amusing anecdotes about certain individuals such as the brother of one of their acquaintances – he, it was said, could hear bats.

Julia's teasing of Edward leads him to explain his wife's absence from the cocktail party. He claims that she is away visiting an aunt. The drift of the conversation shows that Julia does not believe his story. However, she does not choose to press him at this moment. Instead, she invites him to a dinner-party at her house the following Friday. She decides to leave at that point, and the others follow.

The Unidentified Guest, however, agrees to keep Edward company a little longer. At this point Edward apologises for the failure of the party and explains how it came about. He says he was particularly troubled about Julia, whom he both fears and dislikes. At this important juncture Julia reappears – in search of her umbrella. Having retrieved it, she again makes her exit, but not before remarking that the two of them are plotting something. When they are once again alone, Edward confesses to his Unidentified Guest that his wife has left him. The Guest immediately assumes an air of authority. He mixes Edward a drink, and begins to interrogate him. Edward objects but the stranger insists on describing what may be Edward's reactions to his wife's departure. He suggests, for example, that Edward may gradually come to welcome her absence and find his life more comfortable without her. Edward rejects this suggestion and says he feels disturbed by her leaving him without any explanation. The mystery of it is disconcerting. In response to this, the stranger suggests that we often need these sudden shocks to take stock of ourselves and make us realise what we really are. We begin, he says, to examine ourselves and our identity. The humiliation that we may sometimes suffer on such occasions can be an invaluable experience.

Edward seems driven to despair. He cannot give any real reason for wanting his wife back – he only knows that he needs her. It is then that the action takes a surprising turn. For the Unidentified Guest assumes an even greater air of authority and assures Edward that his wife *will* return on condition that he will ask no questions about where she has been. The ringing of the doorbell at this point might suggest to the audience that it is, indeed, Edward's wife returning. Instead it proves to be Julia and Peter. Julia claims she has returned to look for her glasses. Their return is a cue for the exit of the Unidentified Guest who leaves singing a song about 'One Eyed Riley'.

Julia takes exception to the song, which she thinks is directed at her. Being inquisitive, she wants to know everything about the stranger and what has been happening at the flat in her absence. She hazards a guess that his name is Riley – referring here to the words of the song he had been singing – proving remarkably accurate, as will be seen later. Having found her glasses, Julia leaves again. Peter stays behind to talk to Edward. He confides in Edward and tells him of his love for Celia and her apparent growing indifference to him. It is now Edward's turn to assume the role of counsellor to Peter just as the Unidentified Guest had counselled him. The advice he gives is the same: do nothing. Peter's outpourings to Edward are interrupted by the return of yet another of the guests, namely Alex. He has come back to cook Edward's dinner, and Peter's sad confession is punctuated by enquiries about such mundane things as pots and pans or curry powder and eggs. Finally, both Peter and Alexander leave Edward alone. The scene closes with his making a vain attempt to contact Celia by phone.

COMMENTARY: The scene opens at the cocktail party. We have the immediate impression that the party has been going on some time, for the whole atmosphere is relaxed and obviously stories are being freely exchanged. The trivial nature of these exchanges is clearly designed to indicate the superficial nature of the kind of conversation to be expected at a cocktail party. Eliot wants us to recognise that people are concentrating on appearances and not on the real substance of things. The stories that are told, or, more accurately, never told, help to highlight this feature. Having tantalised her audience about Lady Klootz and having been encouraged to finish the story about her, Julia blithely responds with: 'What Lady Klootz?'

In the first part of the scene Edward is at pains to hide the fact that his wife has left him. All must be sacrificed to appearances. He must observe the proper social code. Just as he is about to launch into an attack on the absent Julia, she returns and he has to resume the mask of politeness.

This opening scene is a delightful comedy of manners in which Eliot shows us the upper middle-class 'at play'. Only when those who represent this class have gone can truths be revealed to the anonymous guest. In addition to the comedy of manners, there is a lot of verbal comedy, too. The badinage between the various characters, the ridiculously super-fluous details about various socialites, and the barbs directed by Julia at Edward all add up to a considerable comic effect. This is particularly enhanced by the character of Julia Shuttlethwaite. She dominates the scene from the start and we are reminded repeatedly of her insatiable curiosity. It is this trait that persuades her to return to Edward's flat on two occasions on the pretext of searching for lost objects. She it is who tantalises the rest of the guests with the story of Lady Klootz. And she makes Edward feel so uncomfortable about his missing wife, Lavinia, and his vain efforts to provide food at the cocktail party that has been forced on him.

Food provides the focus for further comedy in this scene when Alex returns to Edward's flat in order to cook him a meal. The comedy is provided not only by Alex's frustration about inadequate facilities in the kitchen but also by Edward's annoyance at his intrusion. Further comedy is created by Alex's banal enquiries cutting into Peter Quilpe's confession of his unrequited love for Celia Coplestone.

In addition to the comedy there is a serious side to the scene. Eliot is concerned with the theme of self-discovery, and this is the function of the exchanges between Edward and the Unidentified Guest. The latter acts as a kind of conscience for Edward. He voices feelings which Edward would perhaps be afraid to admit despite their presence in his nature. In doing so, he forces Edward to examine his real feelings about Lavinia and her desertion. The salutary effect on Edward is almost immediate, for we find that he is able to counsel Peter Quilpe in much the same way as he had been counselled by the Unidentified Guest.

The scene allows us, too, to see the dramatist at work. He uses various dramatic devices to keep his audience guessing and to surprise them. We have, for example, the obvious device of using the anonymous Unidentified Guest. We have, too, the presence of Julia, through whom the playwright asks the questions the audience would like to ask. The pace of the dialogue is skilfully handled to reflect the nature of the action on stage. Thus, when Eliot is keen on creating the effect of idle chatter within a cocktail party he provides rapid exchanges between the various characters. The more serious problems which are aired in the latter part of the scene are given expression in lengthier verse passages. There is, too, plenty of activity on stage, plenty of exits and entrances which help to add considerable variety to the scene. Thus, for example, where Peter is pouring his soul out to Edward his lament is constantly interrupted by Alex's incursions from the kitchen. We also have the beginnings of a plot sketched out in this opening scene. The complications of the lives of Edward, Lavinia, Celia and Peter are already in evidence and waiting to be developed.

NOTES AND GLOSSARY:

Maharaja:	title given to some princes in India
tit-bit:	tasty morsel of food
scenario:	outline of the plot, characters and events of a film
an annuity:	insurance for a yearly payment of money
give me notice:	tell me she was leaving my employment
poke into other people's business:	enquire about other people's affairs in an objectionable manner
genie out of the bottle:	in Arabian tales a spirit was often depicted as being held captive in a bottle
St Anthony:	a Catholic saint said to be helpful in the recovery of lost property
a salon:	a regular meeting-place of artistic and literary figures
a double boiler:	a kitchen utensil consisting of a pan within a pan
a society column:	part of a newspaper that deals with people in the higher levels of society
mangoes:	yellowish-red fleshy tropical fruit, often used in pickles
Montenegro:	a republic in south-east Yugoslavia

Act I   Scene 2

The emotional involvement between Celia and Edward is made clear at the beginning of this scene. Edward's failure to reach her by telephone at the end of Scene 1 is explained by Celia's arrival at his flat fifteen minutes later. She was already on her way when he telephoned. At the same time, she does make some reference to his manner on the telephone and we are thus reminded of a call which interrupted Edward in the previous scene and which obviously disturbed him. Celia is surprised at his unwelcoming attitude now. She wants to be reassured that he still loves her, and tries to persuade him that Lavinia has left him for good. She thinks of Lavinia's departure as a simple way for them to declare their relationship to the world. They can now be married since, she anticipates, Lavinia will give grounds for divorce. However, she has reckoned without the influence of the Unidentified Guest on Edward. He is now already a changed man. Celia cannot understand it. She attributes it all to some devious scheme on Lavinia's part but Edward assures her that the reason lies in their own furtive behaviour.

At this moment, their conversation is interrupted by a telephone call from Alex enquiring about Edward's dinner. The meal Alex had prepared had quite slipped Edward's memory and Celia sets about redeeming the over-cooked food. Edward is anxious that they should not be found in a compromising position. Celia assures him that her cooking for him will appear altogether innocent. She is determined, it seems, to have their affair out in the open. At this moment the arch-gossip and scandal-monger Julia makes her appearance. She claims that she, like Celia, has returned to prepare something to eat for Edward. In her dominant manner she takes over that task and leaves Celia and Edward to their discussion. Edward confesses to Celia that he wants Lavinia to come back. Celia attributes this change of heart in him to the influence of the Unidentified Guest who, she feels, 'has some sort of power'.

Their conversation is once again interrupted by Julia who brings in a half-bottle of champagne. She suggests they drink to Lavinia's aunt! Then she tries to persuade them both to go home with her for supper, but only Celia accepts. First, though, she requests a private conversation with Edward, and we note that Julia guesses that its subject will be Lavinia. When they are once again alone together, Celia insists on knowing how Edward had been persuaded to want Lavinia to return. He is not sure he was persuaded. He feels he made his own decision. Celia chides him for being weak and promises him she will make it all worthwhile for him when they are together. When Edward tells her of Riley and the song he sang she expresses the opinion that Edward is near a nervous breakdown.

She tries once more to make him change his mind, but he is determined to have Lavinia back. Celia accuses him of treating her as simply a diversion and he, in turn, claims that she must have treated Peter Quilpe in the same manner. Celia is enraged at the suggestion, and declares that she never had any love for Peter.

Their lovers' quarrel then takes a more serious turn. Celia wants to understand Edward, and this prompts him to try to put into words what is happening to him. He claims that he is not master of his own fate. He has begun to feel the presence of a stronger 'self'. Celia echoes that feeling and claims that he has, indeed, changed. The change in him, she says, has begun to effect a change in her, too. She realises that she mistook him for something greater that she would feel forced to aspire to. She is beginning to search now for something which will give more meaning to her life.

At this moment the telephone rings. Their profound thoughts are interrupted by the trivia of Julia's glasses yet again. Once more she claims to have lost them. They are, in fact, found in the kitchen and Celia agrees to take them to her. Before she leaves, she and Edward decide to drink a toast to 'the Guardians'. Edward had already used the word to describe his other self, and now it seems to have assumed a more physical reality in the form of Julia.

COMMENTARY: A sense of continuity is gained by Eliot in the use of Celia as a link between Scene 1 and Scene 2. The previous scene had ended with Edward's telephone call to her and the present scene opens with her appearance. We note immediately the sense of furtiveness, of the clandestine, and it is quickly confirmed that Edward and Celia have been having an illicit love-affair. It is with the resolution of this love-affair that this scene deals. Both characters experience a change of attitude and, indeed, a change of self, a wish for higher things. They are bemused by the reasons for this change in them and attribute it, quite spontaneously, to what they choose to call 'the Guardians'. This notion is crucial in the play. Edward had already used the term to describe his other self but it takes on a more visible form in the shape of Julia, and Alex and the Unidentified Guest. These three are part of the mystery of the play. They are the visible presences of the spirit world which guides men's destinies. In this scene, Edward expresses the feeling that the course of his life had been set long ago, and the Guardians will come to add more conviction to that feeling. Celia had earlier voiced her sense that the Unidentified Guest was more than a man: she senses the power in him, and is afraid.

This use of the spirit world visiting mankind to set them right was not new in twentieth-century English drama. Just three years before Eliot's play was performed at the Edinburgh Festival, J. B. Priestley (b.1894) had used the same device in a play called *An Inspector Calls*. There an Inspector Goole (Priestley's pun on 'ghoul' meaning a visiting spirit, usually with an evil intent) calls on a group of people and disturbs their consciences. His major purpose is to awaken in them a greater sense of responsibility. (We learn later that no such person as Inspector Goole exists.) The parallel between Eliot's play and Priestley's is made even clearer by the fact that in each play it is a young woman who benefits most by the visitation – Celia in Eliot's play, Sheila in *An Inspector Calls*.

The greater part of this scene has a serious intent, but there is still plenty of comedy in it. Julia's presence ensures that. Here she resumes her role as a busybody, and continues to tease Edward about Lavinia's imaginary aunt. The feeding of Edward once again offers some splendid comical moments, and we have some wonderful exchanges between Julia and Edward about the dish that Alex had prepared for him. Eliot uses the telephone as a device to interrupt serious passages in the scene. He uses Alex's call about the meal he had cooked to break into the initial argument between Celia and Edward, and then a call from Julia to stop any further discussion between the two. The role of Julia and Alexander as Guardians is thus becoming clearer. They *are* guiding the action. The pattern of the scene is quite similar to that adopted in Scene 1. Initially we have comedy, then serious conversation, and finally a light ending to the scene. Eliot likes to use the various interruptions to the serious parts of the scene to create a feeling of suspense. The two characters in this scene intent on a serious confrontation are frustrated in their attempts to discuss their problems. This adds to their sense of frustration and, at the same time, keeps the audience alert as it waits for the next episode.

Notice that in this scene Eliot gives voice, through Celia, to his philosophic concern about the difference between appearance and reality. She thinks that her idea of love had been real, but now it seems it was only a dream. She says,

Perhaps the dream was better. It seemed the real reality,
And if this is reality, it is very like a dream.   (p. 65)

In these lines Eliot sums up the difficulties the human being has in dealing with these two concepts. The difficulties involved in making the distinction between the two are given visible form through the presence of the Guardians. Are they real people? Or are they spirits? Or are they both? Within this scene, too, Eliot gives Edward a lengthy speech in which he examines his 'self', his real identity. Here he risks losing his audience who may be reluctant to try to follow the density of Edward's reasoning. Critics have generally praised Eliot for abstaining from such lengthy philosophising as occurs in Edward's speech in which he tells us that:

if there is any happiness,
Only the happiness of knowing
That the misery does not feed on the ruin of loveliness,
That the tedium is not the residue of ecstasy.   (p. 68)

Despite the threat of tedium prompted by such a speech, Sean Lucy, for example, claims that 'the play compels our interest on the stage and is never in danger of becoming tedious. It is what critics call "good theatre" – so good that it entertains even those who do not understand it.'*

NOTES AND GLOSSARY:

Good Samaritans: a reference to Christ's story in the New Testament (Luke 10:30–7) of the man from Samaria (that is, a Samaritan) who helped a Jewish stranger who had been robbed and beaten. The Samaritan paid for him to be looked after in an inn. For his act of kindness the Samaritan is seen as a symbol of charity

---

Act I   Scene 3

The Unidentified Guest returns the next day to the Chamberlaynes' flat. He has no purpose in doing so except to remind Edward that he had made a decision. He tells Edward that the decision affected his free will unalterably. The decision he made the day before is something he cannot change now for his moment of choice has passed. At that point in time, he tells Edward, he had set in motion forces which could affect his own life, and those of others, irreversibly. The Unidentified Guest speaks of the nature of time and experience. Because of the nature of time the person

*Sean Lucy, *T. S. Eliot and the Idea of Tradition*, Cohen and West, London, p. 197.

we meet at one point will be the same person *to us* when we meet him again. However, in reality he cannot be exactly the same to himself because of the many things he will have experienced in the meantime. We are, in fact, according to that reasoning, always strangers to one another.

Strange things are about to happen. People are drawn to the flat in mysterious ways. First Celia arrives, under orders from Julia; then Peter appears, under orders from Alex. Both Julia and Alex claim that Lavinia had sent them a telegram asking them to meet her at the flat. When Lavinia arrives there, however, she knows nothing of the telegram she is supposed to have sent. Nor does she know anything about a sick aunt or about being in Essex. She feels confused, feeling that reality is playing strange tricks with her:

> But it seems to me that yesterday
> I started some machine, that goes on working,
> And I cannot stop it . . .   (pp. 88–9)

She is in exactly the same position as Edward, according to the Unidentified Guest. Just as he had told Edward that his 'moment of freedom' has passed, so Lavinia now complains that she does not feel free. The flat is briefly full of people. First Celia and Peter are there to disclose their separate intentions of leaving the country. Then they are joined by Alex and Julia both of whom refuse to explain the mystery of the telegrams. They both act quite strangely and assertively. Yet Eliot allows them one light touch of comedy. Julia points out that Lavinia is, no doubt, hungry after her long journey. Alex is immediately about to offer his services as a cook when Julia steps in to save Lavinia from that fate. Prompted by her, they all leave Edward and Lavinia alone.

The initial exchanges between these two are awkward for they have both been instructed to ask no questions and offer no explanations. After the busy conversation of the early part of the scene silence seems about to descend. Then Lavinia shows real strength of character in offering an apology to Edward. She says how sorry she is to have left him to deal with the cocktail party she had arranged. She is eager to know how Edward dealt with the awkward situation.

Having found a way of talking to each other they quickly fall to attacking one another. They begin by complaining about their life together over the past five years. Lavinia complains that Edward was reluctant to make decisions and it was she who had to be forceful. Edward complains that she was too forceful and domineering, that she wanted him merely to contribute to her social life, that she treated him almost as a domestic servant. Having abused one another, they wonder why they have come together again. It is something they cannot explain; Lavinia feels that something made her come back. Both agree that they will behave differently to one another in the future. They do not mean this in any conciliatory sense. What they mean is that neither will allow the other to gain any advantage. But they immediately begin to try to gain just such an advantage. Lavinia taunts Edward, claiming that he likes to pretend that he is capable of maturing. She is convinced he will never change for the better. Edward is quite annoyed with her for her complacency, for thinking she knows him better than he knows himself. Lavinia, for her part, takes exception to the fact that he never seems interested enough in her to want to know her.

Having abused one another they feel that, at least, they are actively engaged in something. The difference between this and their previous relationship is that before they were quite indifferent to one another. This seems to act as an invitation to more hard-hitting remarks. Edward protests at being treated by her as immature. His tone and manner become much more serious. He feels that he is somehow doomed to a life completely devoid of happiness.

Lavinia expresses the opinion that Edward is heading for a nervous breakdown and we remember that Celia had the same idea in Act I, Scene 2. We remember, too, that earlier in this present scene Celia had laughed at Edward because he was behaving like a little boy about to be punished by the headmaster. Both women adopt this superior attitude towards him, and he addresses them both when he speaks of happiness having deserted him for ever. Both women have in mind an excellent doctor who could cure him. When Lavinia suggests treatment Edward is even more alarmed. He claims that the only cure for him is for time to be turned back twenty-four hours so that he could revoke the decision he appears to have taken. For now, he says, he is living a nightmare inhabited by such beasts as the python and the octopus. Lavinia has the last word. She reduces everything to the trite and the ordinary by speaking, once again, of having a meal, and in the last line of this scene she provides evidence of using Edward as a servant when she asks him to have a meal brought up.

COMMENTARY: In the commentary on Scene 2, mention was made of Eliot's readiness to introduce into his play some philosophical lines of thought that might well be incomprehensible to some members of his audience. There is an instance of this early in Scene 3. There, the Unidentified Guest introduces the issue of free will to make one's own decisions and warns that the privilege of free will carries with it the responsibility of abiding by one's decision. In addition, he also introduces a perspective on human identity. He suggests we often take for granted that, when we meet one another after an absence, we are actually the same person greeting the person we knew. He is of the mind that in both cases a real change will have occurred by nature of the laws of existence.

Both these notions of free will and identity are key issues in the consequent events in this scene. Eliot lays here the philosophical groundwork on which the rest of the scene is to be built. The interaction between Edward and the Unidentified Guest is made to resemble the exchanges – to be found in folk tales and myths – between a mortal and some supernatural or preternatural being who has come to deliver a message of some gravity. As the 'vision' threatens to disappear, the visionary appeals for it to remain and reveal more. Here Edward exclaims: 'Stop! Will you come back with her?' (p. 76). Edward is a willing believer. He accepts the Unidentified Guest uncritically. It is a mark of Eliot's dramatic skill that we, too, have come to accept both his presence and his pronouncements so willingly. He has, of course, already made us ready to understand this stranger.

The variety of pace and incident already experienced in the play encourages us to accept these quiet passages as a necessary part of the structure. The exit of the Unidentified Guest acts as a cue for a change of pace as the stage becomes a setting for various comings and goings. It seems that the unexpected, the surprise, is Eliot's main aim in the central part of this scene.

The various arrivals have been prompted by mysterious messages which Alex and Julia claim to have received. These two are assuming a role rather like that of the Unidentified Guest. They have a real physical presence in the play, but are capable of manipulating events by virtue of some special gifts. We begin to notice how they can interrupt proceedings at exactly the moment of their own choosing, and, of course, it is they who are instrumental in bringing Celia and Peter back to Edward's flat. Julia has already proved herself to be a dominant force in the play, and her influence is singled out for special mention by a puzzled Lavinia:

That woman is the devil.
She knows by instinct when something's going to happen.   (p. 91)

This is the first scene in the play in which Lavinia appears. Eliot has prepared us for her, but her actual presence persuades us that she is a real force for Edward to contend with. We know already that all is not well between them. She had left him abruptly and put him in a very embarrassing position, having to deal with inquisitive guests at a pre-arranged cocktail party. She had driven him to invent the lie that she had gone to visit a sick aunt in Essex. When she returns, she is initially repentant. She apologises for putting him in an awkward predicament. Her tone, however, quickly changes and she attacks him fiercely as a weak and indecisive man. Edward had said to Celia that he could never be happy with Lavinia, and this scene helps to show us why.

The scene is one that seems very much conerned with the struggle to be happy. The notion of happiness is synonymous in Eliot's terms with self-realisation, with being able to make the right decision, abiding by it, and through that achieving a state in which worthwhile personal achievement is possible. Edward, in this scene, bitterly resents the decision he made and his responsibility to keep to it.

The final scene in the play will show that his courage will bring him true happiness. His initial reaction, however, *is* one of terror, and this is expressed, if only briefly, in his references to the python and the octopus. This kind of image is not unexpected in Eliot. There are outstanding instances of similar usages in his earlier play *Murder in the Cathedral*. There the Chorus, anticipating the beginning of tragedy, express their fear of what is to come in a series of images like these:

> The forms take shape in the dark air:
> Puss-purr of leopard, footfall of padding bear,
> Palm-pat of nodding ape, square hyena waiting*

In that play, too, the notion of free will, of the need to make the right decision and abide by it, is stressed repeatedly and insistently. There, however, the greatest achievement in man is seen in reaching that state where his will is the same as that of God. As Thomas of Canterbury, Eliot's hero in *Murder in the Cathedral*, puts it:

> the true martyr is he who has become the instrument of God, who has lost his will in the will of God, and who no longer desires anything for himself, not even the glory of being a martyr.   (Interlude, ll. 67–70)

These words come from Thomas of Canterbury's sermon, and it is to a sermon that one critic has compared the action in *The Cocktail Party*. T. S. Matthews wrote:

> Christopher Fry's† *The Lady's Not for Burning*, resolutely rhetorical and purposefully poetic, was also playing to full houses in New York at the same time. Fry's simple meaning could be cheerfully swallowed whole, whereas Eliot's dark hints stuck in the gullet like a bone.‡

However, in defence of Eliot, it must be said that the action in this scene, and, indeed, in the whole of this first act is in direct contrast to the static impact of a sermon. What Matthews is trying to suggest is that Eliot's play made people feel guilty about being self-centred and selfish.

NOTES AND GLOSSARY:

Great Eastern: a reference to a railway company operating in eastern England up to 1923

*T. S. Eliot, *Murder in the Cathedral*, Part 1, ll. 658–60.

†Christopher Fry (*b.* 1907), English dramatist famous for his witty verse plays like *The Lady's Not for Burning* (1949).

‡T. S. Matthews, *Great Tom, Notes Towards the Definition of T. S. Eliot*, Weidenfeld and Nicolson, London, 1973, pp. 167–8.

Act II

This act can usefully be divided into five sections. The first shows Sir Henry Harcourt-Reilly preparing to deal with Edward, Lavinia, and Celia. A second involves Reilly's private interview with Edward; a third consists of his interview with Edward and Lavinia together; the fourth section is his private interview with Celia. The fifth and last section is the strange meeting of Sir Henry, Alex, and Julia.

The preparations for the various interviews are made in a very precise manner. Yet the whole thing is shrouded in mystery. The audience may well already be puzzled by the reappearance of the Unidentified Guest as Sir Henry Harcourt-Reilly, a consultant psychiatrist. They are left equally puzzled initially about the identity of his three patients. When Alex appears on the scene, it might well be thought he is the first patient, but he reveals to us that it is Edward who is due to arrive. It is Alex, too, who provides further insight into Edward's character in telling us that he likes being ill. Edward is both attention-seeking and self-centred. At the same time, Sir Henry offers us his opinion that Edward's apparent masochism is really a form of escape from responsibility, as well as an attempt to gain an advantage over his wife. The reference to Lavinia is probably humorous, but that to Edward's selfishness is certainly not.

On his arrival, Edward is at once defensive and aggressive. He protests that the decision to have his wife back was forced on him by Reilly, while he was in no condition to make any decisions himself. Reilly does not treat him altogether gently. He points out that Lavinia's return had saved at least one life (here he is referring to Celia), and that he and Lavinia could still avoid disaster. He tells Edward outright that he is too impetuous and points out that the decision is really out of his hands.

Sir Henry even insults him by referring slightingly to his intellectual capability. Edward volunteers the opinion that he had wished his wife to return because she had created a need in him. She had so possessed him that he lacked any real personality. She had emasculated him:

I cannot live without her, for she has made me incapable
Of having any existence of my own.   (p. 112)

He begs Reilly to send him to a sanatorium where he can be alone. He has endured real agony of spirit, he says, much worse than any physical pain. He feels he has lost all power to act, and that he is completely in Reilly's hands. Reilly sees all of this as self-indulgence on Edward's part. Edward is enjoying his disturbed state. That being the case, Reilly takes matters into his own hands. He tells Edward that he is no longer free, but that freedom is something for Sir Henry to grant or not, as he decides.

As a show of his strength Sir Henry now brings in Lavinia to face Edward. During the ensuing discussion we learn that Sir Henry was responsible for her disappearance at the beginning of the play. He had been acting as her psychiatrist and recommended a rest for her at what she thought was a sanatorium. Lavinia is not pleased to learn that it was a hotel, not a sanatorium and asks rather heatedly: 'Are you a devil/Or merely a lunatic practical joker?' (p. 116).

We remember that she had earlier referred to Julia as a devil, too: the links between Reilly and Julia are becoming clearer. Reilly points out that in order to enter his sanatorium one would need to have 'an honest mind'. We later learn that only those who are saints are seen as fit to enter that sanatorium.

Lavinia and Edward, according to Reilly, are far from honest – they lied to him in that they told the truth only so far as it pleased them to do so. He discloses Edward's affair with Celia. That comes as no surprise to Lavinia. Then he does take Edward by surprise by telling of the liaison between Lavinia and Peter Quilpe. Sir Henry uses both love affairs to demonstrate to Edward and Lavinia respectively that they are ideally suited to one another. In the failure of their two affairs, they discovered the real truth about themselves. Edward realised that he was not really capable of loving anyone, and Lavinia that no one could really love her. They had come to see that they were isolated, and Reilly points out that to go to his 'sanatorium' would only have aggravated that condition for both of them.

His counsel pushes Edward and Lavinia closer together and they seek a reconciliation. Edward shows concern for the ruin he may have brought on other people, and this expression of concern indicates his maturing in the course of the play. Reilly explains that one cannot hope to deal with problems which are beyond one's control. Lavinia sees the point of this in the light of what Reilly had said about free choice. Those others had made their choice just as Edward and Lavinia had.

There is a short interlude between the Chamberlaynes' departure and the entry of Celia. During this interlude we are shown something of the relationship between Julia and Reilly. They are obviously equals, but Julia seems to be somehow dominant. Reilly feels exhausted after his interview with Edward and Lavinia and wishes to rest. Julia prompts him into further action.

The interview with Celia reveals something of her background to the audience. She comes from an old wealthy family which has now lost most of its wealth. They live in the country. Celia lives in a flat in London with a cousin who is temporarily abroad. Celia finds that her greatest affliction at the moment is that of being alone and yet seeing no reason why she should *not* be alone. She sees solitude as an inevitable human condition, and is concerned whether this is truly so. Her other concern is about 'a sense of sin'. This seems to her to go totally against her upbringing in which the supernatural was never even acknowledged. Being immoral, doing anything wrong, was simply seen as acting against a social code. At the same time, one would be persuaded to assume an indifferent air to such misdemeanours for to begin to care about them would be seen as abnormal.

Celia feels driven by her 'sense of sin' to make recompense, to 'atone', as she puts it. She feels as though she had been seeking something valuable in her relationship with Edward and now feels guilty at not having achieved it. She wants to be cured of this feeling of loss and failure. Reilly points out that the cure must lie in her own decision. He can offer two ways toward a cure. One is simply to teach her how to accept 'the human condition'. This would enable her to live with the memory of the past and to deal with the daily routine.

The other is more heroic, he says, for it entails a continuing struggle with the self. It is a demanding search for the reality that Celia had always wanted. It is the way of the saints, and it is the way that Celia chooses. She says that she does not know why she has chosen it but realises the important factor: it is *her* decision. Reilly assures her that she has done it for 'the best reason' – an important statement in Eliot's terms. Reference has already been made to his earlier play *Murder in the Cathedral* (1935) and to its hero, Thomas of Canterbury. He tells us that

> The last temptation is the greatest treason:
> To do the right deed for the wrong reason.*

Celia, like Thomas, will go on to become a Christian martyr, and, to quote Thomas again: 'the true martyr is he who has become the instrument of God, who has lost his will in the will of God, and who no longer desires anything for himself'.†

These lines describe Celia's state perfectly. She is to go to Reilly's sanatorium, where only a select few can enter. After Celia has gone, Julia returns and it is ironic to see the counsellor being counselled. Edward had earlier expressed concern for 'the others' and Reilly had set his mind at ease. Now Reilly himself says, 'It's the other ones I am worried about' (p. 142), and he in his turn is reassured by Julia. His other ones are Edward and Lavinia, and Julia reminds him that they themselves made their decisions and must abide by them. Julia, as was originally suggested, seems a dominant force necessary to Reilly. He does not fully understand what he has done, even to the extent of not understanding the form of words he used when bidding farewell to Edward and Lavinia, and Celia: 'Work out your salvation with diligence.' Yet it is Reilly who leads the subsequent chants or prayers that accompany what they call 'the libation'. This is, literally, a drink offering to the gods. The first prayer is for Edward and Lavinia and expresses the hope that they can build up a

---

*T. S. Eliot, *Murder in the Cathedral*, Part 1, ll. 667–9.
†T. S. Eliot, *Murder in the Cathedral*, Interlude, ll. 67–70.

happy home – this is the 'hearth' that is referred to. The second prayer is for Celia who is setting forth on her 'terrifying journey'.

There is a fourth person for whom they cannot pray as yet, namely, Peter Quilpe. But the end of this scene holds out a promise for him as well, because there are 'guardians', as Alex says humorously, even in California.

COMMENTARY: This act helps to explain why Eliot had originally intended to call the play *One-Eyed Riley*, for Sir Henry Harcourt-Reilly certainly proves to be central to this middle act in the play, even if one critic has said of *The Cocktail Party* that 'the exceptional individual is no longer in the foreground or in the centre of the design'.* Reilly's role in this act can be seen as challenging such a statement. It is he who largely controls the actions in this part of the play, and it is to him that Edward, Lavinia, and Celia look for help, encouragement and guidance.

His all-powerful effect is somewhat offset by his strange lack of self-assurance towards the end of the act, as well as by Julia's admonitions to him earlier to resist tiredness. Yet this serves more to emphasise her role than to diminish that of Reilly. She, like both Reilly and Alex, has been an ambiguous figure throughout the play. In this act, however, we begin to see the reality showing through. Alex indicates that the same powers that are exercised by them can be shown by others as far away as California. The impression is of a spiritual link, an impression that has already been created by the incantations and 'libations' that preceded Alex's remark. The fact that these three are not human is implied even earlier by Julia when she says to Reilly:

But what do we know of the terrors of the journey?
You and I don't know the process by which the human is
Transhumanised   (p. 144)

This last word is suggestive of the spiritual existence towards which the chosen few are seen to aim. In this play, it is Celia who represents the saints in humankind, who speaks of recognition of 'sin'. She finds it difficult to define her understanding of the concept of sin but she sees it as having more serious implications than merely doing wrong to her fellow-man. It is on a higher plane than that. She sees the need to 'atone' for sin, and, in that choice of word, identifies herself with a Christian view of crimes committed by man against God. Her use of the word assumes even greater significance later in her death. She dies by crucifixion, the method of atonement used by Christ in his payment for men's sins.

It is useful to think of the word 'atonement' in another shape, namely as 'at-one-ment', for this search for self-realisation, for achieving peace

*D. E. Jones, *The Plays of T. S. Eliot*, Routledge and Kegan Paul, London, 1960, p. 130.

within oneself, is at the heart of this act and of the entire play. Different paths towards this goal may be taken, as Reilly remarks. Edward and Lavinia are to seek it in mutual toleration, while for Celia the journey towards this state will be more difficult and will involve a more painful awareness of being alone. Notice how Eliot likes to play with paradox here. Reilly tells Celia: 'Each way means loneliness – and.communion' (p. 139).

Such concern with the possible meanings of words and their various associations offers some justification for our seeing more than the surface meaning of such a word as 'atonement'. Eliot obviously finds satisfaction in such word-play. It is basic to his philosophising which dominates Act II and distinguishes it from the other two. The philosophising need not be on an altogether serious level all of the time – we are reminded more than once by the language that this *is* a comedy. Humour can also be found in the marital exchanges between Lavinia and Edward, and especially in Edward's surprise on discovering that his clandestine affair with Celia was public knowledge. Even the trinity of Reilly, Julia and Alex have their humorous moments in this act.

Julia's bullying of Reilly is a simple example of this, and another is provided in Alex's final comment in the act. Helen Gardner spoke of them as 'the comic engineers of the plot' and refers in this act to 'the one-eyed Reilly, the psychiatrist who has to lie down on his own couch.'*

In dramatic terms, Eliot still retains the 'exits and entrances' effect that was a feature of the scenes in Act 1. He is fond of this effect of movement and of surprises. He likes to keep the audience asking: who will come next?

Despite this sense of movement, however, this act creates a far more static impression than the rest of the play. Once on stage, the various characters are engaged in lengthy and, at times, complicated exchanges. There are moments of emotion but most of the workings of the act are intellectual. At one point in the act (p. 110), Reilly tells Edward that it would be so simple for him to create a sensational effect which would persuade him that something worthwhile had been achieved. It would, however, be a merely fleeting, transient impression. The appearance would have been there, immediately attractive, but reality would have been lacking. Reilly's words might equally well be addressed by Eliot himself to his theatre audience.

Part of the irony of the play is that Eliot has chosen such a genre in which to present a study of reality versus appearance. For we may well wonder, given the necessary artificiality of the theatre, where reality can ever be seen to lie. The question presents itself most forcibly in this act. It is a question that is particularly pressing in that extraordinary con-

---

*Helen Gardner, 'The Comedies of T. S. Eliot' in *T. S. Eliot, The Man and his Work*, ed. Allen Tate, Chatto and Windus, London, 1967, pp. 169-70.

clusion to the act when the ceremony of libation carries us into quite another area of experience, an area that seems far removed from any reality that any of us have known. The ritual seems to represent a reality familiar enough to the Guardians but one which can be reached only painfully, by a chosen few.

Act III

The curtain rises on a normal world in Act III. The wheel has come full circle for we find that Lavinia is preparing for another cocktail party. There have been a great many cocktail parties since last we met her and Edward, as two years have passed since their meeting with Sir Henry Harcourt-Reilly. Relations between the Chamberlaynes are very amicable indeed. They have learned to live happily with one another and to show consideration for each other's needs. They show a loving concern for one another, and are now able to make jokes without hurting each other.

Their first visitor is Julia. She is the same busy Julia whom we met in the first act. There is, too, a reminder of the Julia who in Act II prevented Reilly from taking his rest. For here, again, she is instrumental in rousing a tired Lavinia. Ever the gossip, Julia brings news that Alex has returned that very day from a mysterious expedition. The mention of his name seems to be a cue for his entry. He discloses that he has just returned from an island in the East called Kinkanja. He does not anticipate that anyone will have heard of it. The island is inhabited by 'heathen' and Christian natives whose different cultures have led to friction and civil war. The hostilities have resulted in murder and cannabalism, and amongst the Christian victims is Celia Coplestone.

The news about Celia is delayed by the entry of Peter Quilpe who has returned from filming in New York. He is 'on location' in England making another film. It is he who is instrumental in evoking the news of Celia's death. For he is looking for Celia to give her a part in his 'film of English life'. In stark contrast to her taking part in an idyll of English country life we are given the detail that 'she must have been crucified/Very near an ant-hill' (p. 169). The revelation shatters Peter completely. He thinks of the two years he spent away from Celia and lost in his world of film as wasted. Now the others point out to him what he can learn about himself from this experience.

Reilly consoles him by reminding him that he is a master of his art. Lavinia tells him to regard the loss of Celia not as an end but as a beginning, a point of view that is echoed by Edward. Julia encourages Peter to look at the death of Celia objectively. This remark prompts Lavinia to comment that Reilly obviously viewed the event objectively for, when he heard of Celia's death, his face 'showed no surprise or horror'. Reilly is quite candid in his explanation of his lack of emotion: the reason is that he foresaw it. At the time of the first cocktail party he had had a vision of the death that awaited Celia. His insistence, as ever, is that her death was the result not of his earlier vision but of her decision and exercise of free will. When Edward and Lavinia express their feelings of guilt about Celia's death, Reilly hastens to stress once more that Celia's death was her own deliberate choice. The more she was aware of it, the more suffering was involved, the more triumphant her death proved.

Now Julia brings the party back to present reality. She indicates that the same design that took Celia off to Kinkanja demands that Peter continue with his film and the Chamberlaynes with their cocktail party. Reilly describes this as their 'appointed burden'. It is hardly a cheering way to anticipate a party but it aptly summarises his way of looking at human activities.

COMMENTARY: *The Cocktail Party* has often been described as a 'well-made play', which usually means a play that has a well-defined beginning, middle and end. This last act does seem designed to tie up loose ends. It provides the audience with information about how the Chamberlaynes fared once they had decided to live together. It gives an account of Peter's career, and, perhaps most significantly, it reports on Celia's fate. In these respects it is possible to see this last act as something linked to the previous two as a kind of Epilogue. Yet it is more than that. At the end of Act II it was said that the task of converting Peter Quilpe remained still to be carried out. The Guardians saw him as the fourth human being who was still to be shown the way. Peter's case, then, is not treated as a mere 'extra' to the action, but is seen as integral to it. So, just as Act II saw the conversion of Edward, Lavinia, and Celia, so this act sees the dawn of Peter's enlightenment. Given that a major theme of this play is the contrast between appearance and reality, it is appropriate that this last act should deal particularly with the man whose professional career is dealing in this contrast, for Peter's career is in films. Film is the medium which deals in illusion. Mention was made earlier of the irony inherent in Eliot's treatment of the conflict between appearance and reality through the medium of the theatre. Film, even more than theatre, deals in illusion, whilst hoping to create an effect of reality. The process of Peter's conversion can be traced through his growing disillusion with his role as a film-maker. Initially, it is the only thing that has meaning for him. The social circles he moves in, rubbing shoulders with such aristocratic families as the Bologolomskys, suits him perfectly. He dines at the 'right' places, and he works for only the best producers, like Bela Szogody.

However, with the news of Celia's death, Peter's world begins to crumble around him. As he puts it: 'That knocks the bottom out of it.' He sees his world, like the film he is making, as second-rate, and worthless.

It is the task, once again, of others like Julia to persuade Peter to view his life differently, to adopt a more mature perspective, to make his choice and abide by it. In Peter's case, this means remaining in the film industry but learning to use that medium for a truer view of reality.

Act III moves at a faster pace than Act II. We have far fewer lengthy speeches and many more brief exchanges, interruptions and flashes of social repartee. Even where individual speeches are longer they can be either witty, like Julia's entry speech, or full of news and excitement, like Alex's narrative of Celia's death and the events leading up to it. Eliot does not offer it as an unbroken narrative but, instead, breaks it up by either the entrance of other characters or simply verbal interruptions. The most outstanding example of creating suspense in Alex's narrative occurs when he is about to tell us about Celia's death. He is interrupted by Peter's entrance and his account is considerably delayed. The news, when given in the end, gains so much more force through Peter's presence. The act provides a contrast to Act II and a close comparison with Act I by its humorous content. The humour can take the form of the witty exchanges between the characters in the early part of the act, or a rather more macabre form as in Peter's statement about having dined at a sophisticated restaurant called the 'Saffron Monkey'. This gains its macabre effect by being mentioned immediately after Alex's detailed account of the eating of monkeys in Kinkanja. The eating of monkeys, in turn, provides a contrast to the more polite and restrained conventions of a cocktail party. These conventions can themselves, though, be very demanding on hosts and hostesses and the play's ending coincides with the end, too, of the cocktail party season. Edward and Lavinia see the end of the season as a merciful release from such pressures. Eliot's audience may well feel a comparable sense of relief after having been forced by the dramatist to examine their own consciences; T. S. Matthews claimed that audiences left the theatre after watching *The Cocktail Party*, beating their breasts and exclaiming 'mea culpa' ('my fault').*

Perhaps Matthews is exaggerating somewhat, but the overall effect of the play is to persuade us to look into ourselves, to introspect, and to say with Lavinia: 'I feel guilty too' (p. 176).

There comes a point in this act when Eliot prompts us to think of our responsibility for our actions once more, by raising the issue of predestination versus free will.

The problem of predestination has always taxed Christian theologians. If, as is argued, God is all-knowing then He must know we are going to 'sin' (to use Celia's word). Given this knowledge why does He not prevent the act that would be a sin? The orthodox answer is that to intervene would affect the exercise of human free will. Reilly raises the issue when

*T. S. Matthews, *op. cit.*, p. 168.

he admits that he foresaw Celia's death. He points out that his fore-knowledge did not make him responsible for the manner of her death. That was her own choice.

NOTES AND GLOSSARY:

a Parkinson party:	Julia means that a firm of caterers called Parkinson will have provided the food for the party
Sultan:	a Muslim ruler
V.A.D.:	Voluntary Aid Detachment
Babylon:	the ancient capital of the Chaldean empire of Southern Mesopotamia
Zoroaster:	Persian prophet; founder of Zoroastrianism which taught that the universe is dominated by opposing forces of good and evil and that good will prevail
Minotaur:	a mythical monster with the body of a man and a bull's head. The king of Crete, Minos, had a labyrinth built to house it

Part 3

Commentary

Eliot's view of drama

Eliot has repeatedly discussed the nature and purpose of drama in his critical writings. The most significant expression of his views on drama is to be found in his essay 'A Dialogue on Dramatic Poetry' written in 1928 and included in his *Selected Essays**. The dialogue is an academic discussion between five anonymous speakers whom we know simply as A, B, C, D, E. Their function is to offer varying and sometimes contrary opinions about the function of drama.

The dialogue opens with the contention that we need to distinguish carefully between the demands made on classical dramatists and those made on modern writers. Reference is made to Aristotle (384–322BC) whose work, *Poetics*, is a classical statement about drama as he knew it. It deals, for example, with such features of drama as the primacy of plot over the depiction of character, the nature of the language used, the nature of tragedy. But Aristotle did not need to concern himself, according to speaker B in Eliot's essay, with such things as 'the relation of drama to religion' or 'the theatre as a paying proposition'. These are considerations at opposite ends of the spectrum yet both are relevant in any discussion of Eliot's views on drama. His concern with religion in his plays is evident. Reference has been made elsewhere in these Notes to his play about the martyr Thomas Beckett, in *Murder in the Cathedral*. In *The Cocktail Party* we are again involved with Christian martyrdom, with sin, with relations between the mortal and the spiritual. An actress, Alison Leggatt, who appeared in *The Cocktail Party* writes: 'I remember one eminent clergyman telling me that the Second Act of *The Cocktail Party* was the finest sermon on Repentance he had ever encountered.'†

While dealing with these highly abstract spiritual themes, Eliot achieved a box-office success, too, in *The Cocktail Party*. By yielding to the demands of realistic drama he made his play 'a paying proposition'.

One way in which, it is claimed, he achieved this was through the structure of the play, by providing a 'beginning, a middle and an end'. In doing this, he made his drama more accessible to his audience. A further aid to popularisation was his use of the comedy form. The play was

*T. S. Eliot, *Selected Essays*, Faber and Faber, London, 1932, pp. 43–58.
†'Postscript on Mrs Chamberlayne and Mrs Guzzard', in: *T. S. Eliot*, ed. Neville Braybrooke, Rupert Hart-Davis, London, 1958, p. 80.

advertised as a comedy, and it has a great many comic ingredients. Julia, for example, is a richly comic character; the marital exchanges of Edward and Lavinia provide plenty of verbal wit and humour; various interruptions of a banal kind on stage are often designed to add light relief and contrast to more serious dialogue. In short, the play is full of comedy.

In his 'Dialogue on Dramatic Poetry', though, Eliot has his speakers attack 'comedy for comedy's sake'. Speaker B asks 'What is the purpose of the theatre except to amuse?' This provokes quite a violent reaction from Speaker E:

> 'It is all very well to reduce the drama to "amusement". But it seems to me that is just what has happened. I believe that the drama has something else to do except to divert us.'   (*Selected Essays*, p. 44)

This leads to an attack on contemporary dramatists such as Sir Arthur Pinero (1855–1934), George Bernard Shaw (1856–1950), and Sir Noel Coward (1899–1973) who sought, according to Speaker C, only to amuse. What they ought to have done, according to him and Speaker B, was 'to assume some moral attitude in common with their audience'. The same speaker might well have been talking of *The Cocktail Party* in a subsequent remark. In applauding a play by the dramatist John Dryden (1631–1700), he tells us that 'It assumes orthodox Christian morality, and laughs [in its comedy] at human nature for not living up to it'.

In saying this he indicates that comedy has a purpose more profound than merely seeking to amuse. The classical understanding of comedy is that, whilst amusing, it would also inculcate a moral stance. The Jacobean dramatist, Ben Jonson (1572–1637), expressed this notion in the introductions to several of his own comedies. In his prologue to *Every Man in his Humour* (1599), for example, he tells us he intends us to laugh at 'errors':

> I mean such errors, as you'll all confess
> By laughing at them, they deserve no less.

In his Preface to his play *Volpone* (1605) he attacks those dramatists who forget the serious moral purpose of comedy and indulge in mere theatrical tricks and cheap jokes:

> the writers of these days are other things; that not only their manners, but their natures are inverted, and nothing remaining with them of the dignity of poet, but the abused name, which every scribe usurps; that now, especially in dramatic or (as they term it) stage-poetry, nothing but ribaldry, profanation, blasphemy, all licence of offence to God and man is practised.

With sentiments like this it is no wonder that Jonson recommended himself to Eliot. In an essay on Jonson written in 1919 and reprinted in

Selected Essays*, he praises him warmly: 'if we had a contemporary Shakespeare and a contemporary Jonson, it might be the Jonson who would arouse the enthusiasm of the intelligentsia'.†

Jonson earns this praise on two particular counts according to Eliot: first, because of the logic of his characters: 'this logic illuminates the actual world, because it gives us a new point of view from which to inspect it'.‡ One major feature of *The Cocktail Party*, too, is just such an insistence on logic. The second feature of Jonson's work that recommends him to Eliot is his poetry, and, again, it may well sound as though Eliot is speaking of himself when he says 'the immediate appeal of Jonson is to the mind'.§

His praise of Jonson's poetry in that essay brings us naturally to Eliot's defence of verse in drama. In his 'Dialogue on Dramatic Poetry' one of his speakers makes the absolute claim that the dramatist must be a poet as well if he is to achieve the highest level of his art. This is the conclusion reached by Speaker D after a lengthy statement by Speaker A about the nature of poetry and drama. The former defends the relevance of verse drama to the modern stage. He refutes the charge of artificiality levelled at drama in verse, pointing out the essential artificiality of any stage production, and upholding the verse form as the natural form for the expression of highest emotions.

It is a spirited defence of what Eliot calls, elsewhere in the essay, the 'question of form'. In *The Cocktail Party* his argument is put into practice through the use of blank verse. Some critics have claimed that the verse could quite as easily have been written in prose form. One of them, as we have already seen in Part 1 of these Notes, suggests the blank verse 'seems to serve only as a kind of notation to assist the actors'**. But this kind of comment is in danger of losing sight of other qualities of the verse form other than those that can be strictly measured. The use of verse has a heightening effect in a variety of ways, not least in the level of language and sentiment adopted by the persons in the drama. It is of a piece, too, with other features of such a play, such as the 'libation' incident in Act II. The verse there changes pace, and form, but given the use of the verse throughout the play this does not do violence to our sensibilities. It seems artistically true in this instance, too, because of the ritual with which it is linked. The ritual is of a religious kind and prompts one to note that in his 'Dialogue on Dramatic Poetry' Eliot traces drama back to religious rites. Speaker E claims that 'drama springs from religious liturgy and it cannot afford to depart far from religious liturgy'.††

*T. S. Eliot, *op. cit.*, pp. 147–60.

†*Ibid.*, p. 159.

‡*Ibid.*, p. 156.

§*Ibid.*, p. 148.

**Bernard Bergonzi, *T. S. Eliot*, The Macmillan Company, New York, 1972, p. 187.

††T. S. Eliot, *Selected Essays*, p. 47.

Religious liturgy is very much concerned with forms and language and can thus easily be seen as relevant to the study of such a play as *The Cocktail Party*. Once critic has said of the verse in the play:

> In *The Cocktail Party*, the verse is verse of the surface, although not superficial. It is conscious lucid statement . . . . It is a very remarkable achievement, for it is both eminently speakable, and also the instrument of complete precision in the expression of feeling.*

It is of interest to compare Williams's assessment of Eliot's verse with Eliot's own statement about the dramatic verse of Ben Jonson:

> the superficies of Jonson is solid. It is what it is; it does not pretend to be another thing.
>
> But it is so very conscious and deliberate that we must look with eyes alert to the whole before we apprehend the significance of any part. We cannot call a man's work superficial when it is the creation of a world: a man cannot be accused of dealing superficially with the world which he has himself created; the superficies *is* the world.†

Structure

The play opens with exactly that effect of superficiality with which we have just been dealing. The opening scene presents a cocktail party in which trivia are being discussed. Stories of no consequence are being told, and social gossip is the order of the day. Yet, even with the gossip and trivia, Eliot is posing questions, creating expectations, and surprises. The sudden disappearance of Lavinia Chamberlayne, for example, is a problem raised early on. Edward Chamberlayne's obvious embarrassment will suggest to the audience that something is amiss. The presence of the Unidentified Guest adds to the sense of mystery. We anticipate that questions asked will be answered, but in the dramatist's own good time and in accord with his intentions. His intentions are best expressed in the words spoken at one point by the Unidentified Guest to Edward. He tells him that the questions will not be answered immediately, but that some benefit will be gained by being made to wait. The gain will be that of personal insight, of coming to know more about oneself:

> There is certainly no purpose in remaining in the dark
> Except long enough to clear from the mind
> The illusion of having ever been in the light.   (p. 37)

It is the function of Act II to grant this self-recognition to three of the 'humans' in the play, namely, Edward, Lavinia, and Celia. Act I is

*Raymond Williams, *Drama from Ibsen to Eliot*, Chatto and Windus, London, 1952, p. 239.
†T. S. Eliot, *Selected Essays*, p. 156.

designed to show us these three in their 'raw' state unaffected by the improving influences they are to experience in Act II. The pace of Act I, in each of its three scenes, is well sustained and characterised by a great deal of activity on stage. Act II is decidedly more quiet, even static, by comparison, given over more to thought than action. The motives behind the actions of the three characters, Edward, Lavinia, and Celia, are the focus of attention.

Act III demonstrates the circular nature of Eliot's design. This act starts with the promise of another cocktail party corresponding to that which was coming to an end in Act I. The circular nature of the play is reflected in the 'round' of parties in which Edward and Lavinia have been involved, and which, they are relieved to say, is coming to an end. Yet, as this act insists, it is their choice to have a cocktail party and to belong to the party-giving society. One critic, Sean Lucy, has claimed that 'the only technical fault' with the structure 'is that the last act is not a last act but an epilogue'.*

However, there are further developments in this last act, including especially the conversion of Peter Quilpe. The act is also necessary, because it demonstrates the new role of counsellor adopted by both Lavinia and Edward. There are necessary links created in Act II with this final act. Alex's final words in Act II, for example, directly signal the return of Peter Quilpe from California. The last act is to be devoted mainly to his conversion. It may seem somewhat unbalanced that this theme is given a whole act, the same length as had been given to the conversion of *three* others. Nevertheless this final act demonstrates the role of those three others in this single conversion.

Themes

Self-identity

The word 'conversion' has been used in describing the workings of the three acts in *The Cocktail Party*. In this context it means the realisation of a new self, a recognition and embrace of what is truly valuable. The term has religious connotations, too, and, in the case of Celia, the coming of true self-knowledge does affect a religious conversion proper. The process of self-discovery is described to Edward by the Unidentified Guest in Act I, Scene 1, as a loss of personality, followed by the realisation of one's true self (pp. 34–6).

It is not surprising that the action takes place at a cocktail party. That is a social occasion of the kind commonly characterised by social courtesies, and light conversation; nothing of any great seriousness. That

*Sean Lucy, *T. S. Eliot and the Idea of Tradition*, p. 197.

is the kind of environment with which the characters involved in this process of self-discovery are familiar. They are not accustomed to soul-searching. They have become complacent and even decadent. Given that background, it is not surprising that Edward is quite astonished to find himself 'confessing' to the Unidentified Guest. He speaks of this confession as a need to relieve his mind and readily admits that the experience is different from what he expected.

For Edward this is the beginning of the process of self-discovery. It is something that must be entered into, no matter how painfully, by each of the 'humans' in the play. It may not be as explicitly described as in the case, say, of Edward, but it is nevertheless a real process for each of them. Celia expresses the agony of it most urgently when, in Act II, she tells Reilly that the gift of self-knowledge is not hers, and that she wants a cure for that complaint however painful that cure might be. Her discovery leads later, literally, to the death of self in martyrdom. It is her example that prompts Peter Quilpe to say that:

> I've only been interested in myself:
> And that isn't good enough for Celia.   (p. 172)

This realisation is the beginning of his own pilgrimage towards self-identity.

Sin

The way towards self-awareness, it was suggested earlier, began with some kind of confession. The confession was, certainly in Edward's case, spontaneous and candid. This notion of confession has religious connotations, too. For the Anglo-Catholic Eliot it would have meant a religious ritual the effect of which purports to be the forgiveness of sin. Sean Lucy has suggested that nowhere in *The Cocktail Party* 'do we get any mention of Christianity or indeed of God'* though he concedes that Celia's entry into a religious order and her martyrdom act as qualifications to this statement.

The theme, though, that really convinces us of the Christian nature of the play is that of Sin. It is a notion that is mentioned by Celia in Act II and is then developed at some length. She identifies it as something of a supernatural nature affecting her relationship with or 'towards someone, or something, outside of myself'. That 'someone' or 'something' is not of this world. Her eventual decision, encouraged by Reilly, to dedicate her life to God indicates that she sees sin as a state of being separated from God – a strictly orthodox Christian belief. The original sacrifice for sin was, in Christian belief, Christ's death on the cross. Eliot

*Sean Lucy, *T. S. Eliot and the Idea of Tradition*, p. 199.

introduces the image into his own play with Celia's crucifixion. Eliot *is* pushing Christianity at his audience. In her interview with Reilly, Celia engages in a dialogue which closely resembles a formal confession of sin. She is expressing repentance for sin and demanding her penance. Acting as her confessor, Reilly offers her two forms of penance, one harsher than the other. She accepts the more harrowing form.

The comedy has a decidedly moral purpose. It is designed to emphasise the moral cowardice of these four humans and their eventual hopes of salvation. Celia's recognition of sin is very much in accord with this moral intent. When she speaks of having 'a sense of sin' Reilly speaks for Eliot's audience in saying 'This is most unusual'. Eliot, admittedly, is not as forthright in his expression of concern for sin as he was, say, in *Murder in the Cathedral*. There are no lines in *The Cocktail Party* to compare with the following which form the conclusion to the earlier play:

> We acknowledge our trespass, our weakness, our fault;
>   we acknowledge
> That the sin of the world is upon our heads; that the
>   blood of the martyrs and the agony of the saints
> Is upon our heads.*

Nevertheless, the role of Celia is so central to the action, and her expression of guilt is so strong, that Eliot's moral intention is equally certain.

Appearance and reality

It is Celia again who provides us with our best evidence of the prominence of this theme in Eliot's play. In the process of her self-discovery she gives voice to her dilemma and predicament. She speaks of the love she had felt, or thought she had felt, for Edward. He had given her sense of reality, she says, a considerable jolt by declaring that their affair was over. Her love for him had, paradoxically, been a dream of reality, and she wishes that she could return to that dream. It is a topic she returns to in Act II when she consults Sir Henry Harcourt-Reilly. She says that she has 'no delusions/Except that the world I live in seems all delusions'. The world, in other words, is one of superficial appearances which serve to cheat and deceive. Celia goes on to bemoan her state and complain about feeling deceived and abandoned. Reilly warns her that indulgence in this kind of disillusionment with the world 'can become itself an illusion'. Eliot obviously enjoys this verbal play, which recurs a little later when Reilly persuades Celia that whichever way of repentance she chooses, 'Each way means loneliness – and communion' (p. 139). The paradox lies in the two words 'loneliness' and 'communion'. At the same time, despite

*T. S. Eliot, *Murder in the Cathedral*, Pt. II, ll. 644–6.

the paradox, the statement is real. It is also effective in helping Celia to

> avoid the final desolation
> Of solitude in the phantasmal world
> Of imagination, shuffling memories and desires.   (p. 139)

The language is strong here and amply demonstrates the threat of such illusion and our becoming slaves to it. In an interview in 1945, Eliot, on being asked about his reaction to the war and its effect on mankind, responded in equally cogent but even more specific terms:

> I should speak of a greater spiritual consciousness, which is not asking that everybody should rise to the same conscious level, but that everybody should have some awareness of the depths of spiritual development and some appreciation and respect for those exceptional people who can proceed further in spiritual knowledge than most of us can.*

Celia can easily be seen as one of those 'exceptional people' who have learned the value of this inner spiritual reality. Her discovery directly affects others, too. The most significant change is in Peter Quilpe who had long admired and loved Celia. He was a man who made his living out of illusions, working as he did in the world of films. He saw it as a medium, as he says, in which he had had to believe, in order to be able to believe in himself (p. 175). With the news of Celia's death his illusions are shattered. He realises he has led a self-centred life and seeks a way to reform. The others give him support. Lavinia and Edward care for him particularly, having themselves experienced something of a growing awareness of reality. Their concern with reality, however, had been in evidence even earlier than the central act. There the commitment to reality began in earnest, but in Act I, Scene 3, Lavinia had already spoken to Edward about her wish to win him away from his illusions. She had told him that she had left him in order to help him towards self-realisation (p. 99). In his own defence Edward protested that he was seeking his own way towards enlightenment and was in no need of her help. It takes Reilly to shock them both into a fresh way of approaching their problems by calling them 'self-deceivers'.

One lesson they must learn is that such self-deceit can only be resolved by conscious decisions on their part. They must *want* to face reality; they cannot be forced into it. Even their interview with Reilly still depends for its effectiveness on their exercise of free will. It is Julia in Act III who warns that, despite their being 'stripped naked to their souls', they might still have recourse to further illusions and the pursuit of false appearances (p. 143).

*'The Condition of Man Today: An Interview with T. S. Eliot', *Horizon*, vol. XII, No. 68, August 1945, p. 88.

Characters

Before considering the characters as individuals we need to consider them in relation to Eliot's source for this play. Reference was made earlier to the Greek writer Aristotle and to his opinion that plot mattered more than character. In Aristotle's view, characters must represent a moral purpose, and this is demonstrably the case with the characters in Eliot's *The Cocktail Party*. Eliot's source was a Greek play by Euripides (484–406BC) called *Alcestis*. The play is named after its heroine who willingly sacrifices her life for the sake of her husband Admetus. Funeral arrangements are under way soon after her death when the son of Zeus, Heracles, arrives. He is on his way to carry out more of the twelve labours imposed on him for his having killed his wife and children. Though mourning for his wife, Admetus carries out his duties as a host and is rewarded by Heracles's restoring Alcestis to life. Admetus may not speak to her, however, for three days. The parallels are quite close in substance. It will be remembered that in Act I, Scene 3, Lavinia speaks of having 'died' for Edward:

> I thought that if I died
> To you, I who had been only a ghost to you,
> You might be able to find the road back
> To a time when you were real   (pp. 98–9)

Sir Henry Harcourt-Reilly (who, like Heracles, is an Uninvited, as well as Unidentified Guest) promises to bring her back. He does not forbid Edward to talk to her, but he does make him promise not to ask her any questions (Act I, Scene 1). He even speaks of bringing her back from the dead. Such a brief outline is of general interest in demonstrating Eliot's source and how true he remains to it. It is of particular interest, too, in highlighting the significant role of Lavinia in the play. It is with her, then, that our study of the various characters will begin.

Lavinia

One critic has drawn not so much a parallel between Alcestis and Lavinia as a contrast. He claims that 'In Alcestis the over-all emphasis is on the spirit of sacrifice . . . . In Lavinia we have only a glimpse of generosity'.* Is it true to think of Lavinia in so grudging a manner? It does seem unfair of her to have abandoned Edward at such an inconvenient time. Yet, as she points out in the lines quoted above (p. 41), her motives were not selfish. She is a woman who does not wish to remain passive. Her attitude towards Edward is, she claims, one of trying to be kind to him. If he fails

*Robert B. Heilman, '*Alcestis* and *The Cocktail Party*', *Comparative Literature*, V (Spring 1955), p. 110.

to respond to that she will try to be deliberately 'horrid' to provoke some reaction in him. She is genuinely anxious for him and is prepared to recommend a psychiatrist to him to help him deal with his threatening nervous breakdown. Edward refuses all offers of help. Later he realises how much he needs Lavinia who, according to him, is possessed of 'obstinate, conscious, sub-human strength'. He realises that life is empty without her. In these perhaps reluctant terms Edward depicts a vibrant, compelling woman.

She is also portrayed by Eliot as very tolerant for she had known of Edward's infidelity throughout his affair with Celia. At the same time, Eliot does not speak of her as entirely good and unselfish. In the first place, as Reilly makes clear, she had falsely pretended to him that it was the discovery of Edward's infidelity that had precipitated the illness about which she consulted him. In addition to this, Reilly reveals that she herself had an illicit affair with Peter Quilpe. Nevertheless, we are left, eventually, with an overall feeling of sympathy for her. Abandoned by Peter who found he was in love with Celia Coplestone, Lavinia felt that no one was able to love her, and she felt isolated.

We find that it is Lavinia who is more ready to repair the relationship between herself and Edward. She it is who suggests a stay at a hotel in the New Forest, and, when Edward says he is too busy, is prepared to accommodate his wishes. These are reasons why we should admire Lavinia and feel sympathy for her. She shows herself capable of such sympathy in the final act of the play when she hears of the tragic death of Celia:

Yet I know I shall go on blaming myself
For being so unkind to her . . . so spiteful.   (p. 176)

This is the kind of act of repentance Eliot is looking for in his characters.

Edward

Eliot's play is concerned with the need for the individual to make decisions, to exercise his free will, and to abide by those decisions and be responsible. It is made clear by Lavinia that Edward's key weakness is this matter of decision-making. She refers, sardonically, to their honeymoon, where the decision about their destination had to be made by her.

It was, for her, the most obvious example of what she describes as passivity on Edward's part. This passivity, she also claims, was a device used by Edward to gain attention. She describes him as self-centred and wishing to have his self-esteem bolstered by others. Again she chooses a humorous example of his selfish concentration on himself. She pictures him as a little boy who would always be measuring himself to show that he had grown (p. 96). This description of Edward by Lavinia occurs in

Scene 3 of Act I. By then we have made Edward's acquaintance. How far does his behaviour corroborate Lavinia's impressions? From the start, it is obvious that Edward is someone of whom people do like to take advantage. Lavinia, having arranged a cocktail party, leaves him to deal with it. He is acutely embarrassed by her absence and this is aggravated by Julia's constant teasing. Edward shows a sad lack of inventiveness in offering the excuse that Lavinia has gone to visit a sick aunt. This lie is easily exposed by Julia.

Our first impression, then, of Edward is certainly that of someone who needs support, who is basically uncertain of himself. In his childhood this lack of self-assurance may well have taken the form of constantly measuring himself as Lavinia suggested. It is Celia who tells Edward quite frankly in Scene 2 of Act I that the excuse he gave for Lavinia's absence was an unconvincing lie. She, too, reinforces the impression we have already gained that Edward is very uncertain of himself socially. When he suggests that he wants Lavinia to come back, Celia's immediate reaction is that he has reached this decision because he was afraid that people would laugh at him, thinking that his wife had left him for another man. However, a new Edward appears at this point in the play, an Edward whom Lavinia had never seen. Celia recognises this change in the decision he makes to bring their affair to an end. So Edward is beginning to learn to make decisions in a way Lavinia had never witnessed. The change in him was effected by his interview with the Unidentified Guest who had told him that it was his duty to find out what his real self is.

Edward feels convinced that he does not function well with other people. He wants to be alone. What he has to learn is to live with other people, to involve himself with them emotionally. The process has to begin with his learning to accept Lavinia, and part of this process is to learn more about himself. Edward proves to be one of Reilly's successes. The last scene of the play reveals a new Edward, outgoing and ready to please others.

Celia

With Eliot's fondness for words and the play of language it is possible that he chose the name Celia for this character because it is derived from the Latin word 'coelum', meaning 'heaven'.

For Celia is the one person in the play who is destined for sainthood. She it is who makes the decision to aim at the highest peak of human perfection and is accepted by Reilly as a guest in his 'sanatorium'. Later, she makes the supreme sacrifice of her life for her faith, dying horribly, 'crucified/Very near an ant-hill'. Celia is Reilly's greatest success story in this play. At the beginning of the play she is a woman who was quite happy to be involved in an adulterous relationship with Edward. On learning that Lavinia has left Edward, she immediately assumes that he will marry her. She has no moral scruples about divorce, nor does she care what society would think of her.

She is obviously a gay, lively socialite. Peter Quilpe finds her sufficiently attractive to wish to become emotionally involved with her. She shows the kindly side to her nature in befriending Peter who seems to be lonely (p. 67).

All in all, Celia seems a perfectly normal, balanced person. Her 'conversion' cannot be attributed to any neurotic tendencies in her. In Edward's case, for example, it might be suggested that he was so impressionable that Reilly could have persuaded him to any course of action. Lavinia, too, we remember, had been under Reilly's psychiatric care. Celia, on the other hand, sees the light even before her interview with Reilly. She suddenly realises that in Edward she had been seeking something that was of great significance to her. Failing to find it in him, she realises her search must continue. She even apologises to Edward for having, in some way, 'used' him:

> The man I saw before, he was only a projection –
> I see that now – of something that I wanted –
> No, not *wanted* – something I aspired to –
> Something that I desperately wanted to exist.   (pp. 69–70)

It is a measure of Celia's will to succeed in her search for perfection that she gains what she aspires to. Her success has its own salutary effects in influencing the minds of others. One significant example of this is Peter Quilpe.

Peter Quilpe

Peter is not central to the action of the play. Indeed, he is absent for much of the time. Yet we notice that even in the central act he is still in the minds of the Guardians as someone whom they still wish to reach. So it is that Peter's part gains more significance in the last act of the play. In the last act he returns to England from California where he had gone to make a career in films as a script–writer. In the first scene of the play we find that he had begun to make a rather hesitant start in this field. In the last act it is clear that he has made some progress, and much of the scene is spent in discussion of his activities. What he has to say indicates that he is very concerned about 'worldly' matters: meeting and pleasing the 'right' people, being seen in all the best, most fashionable places like the 'Saffron Monkey'.

This preoccupation with appearances is aptly illustrated in the career he has chosen. The film medium is a startling example of a world of appearance and illusion. The fragile world he belongs to is quickly shattered, though, by the news of Celia's death. With that news every-thing else loses its purpose and meaning for him.

His experience is not unlike that of Celia herself when she discovered that Edward was no longer available. It made her think more seriously about the meaning of her existence. It was the beginning of her conversion. So it is with Peter. His immediate reaction is to abandon everything, but the other characters in the play tell him that he must be more courageous than that. His change of heart, his self-realisation is almost immediate. He recognises that up to now he has only been interested in himself (p. 172).

The Guardians

Sir Henry Harcourt-Reilly, Julia and Alex constitute a trinity in the play, all intent on one purpose: salvation. They are interested in saving souls. Their wish is for human beings to recognise what is of real value in their lives and to seek for what has real spiritual worth. When Reilly has coun-selled Lavinia and Edward, for example, he is worried that they may simply return to their own trivial ways, concerned with the merely material.

It is the function of the Guardians to help to direct the humans in the play but not to interfere with their exercise of free will. Given their spiritual purpose, it is obvious that their presence will have a mysterious effect. Yet this is not consistently so. It is certainly marked at some points but much less so at others. The most disturbing evidence of their myste-rious nature is provided in the 'libation' scene that concludes Act II. The chanting verses in this scene are reminiscent of the Chorus in Greek drama in which the concern about fate, destiny, spiritual values would find expression.

The 'mystery' connected with the Guardians is clearly demonstrated, too, by the manner adopted by the Unidentified Guest, later known as Sir Henry Harcourt-Reilly. His manner is best described as 'aloof' or 'disinterested'. Under both names, he maintains the impression of being above everything. This is not true, though, of his two colleagues, Julia and Alex. They assume a more obviously human form with more obviously human traits. Julia is the life and soul of any party. She is the busybody, the gossip who could never be described as 'disinterested'. She is also a rich source of humour in the play – which could never be said of Reilly.

Alex, too, makes a measurable contribution to the play in a 'human' kind of way. His culinary schemes in Act I, Scene 1, provide much amuse-ment if not much food. It is Alex, too, who brings the all-important news of Celia's death in the final act of the play. In this last respect, his function reminds us of that of the Messenger in Greek drama whose role was to report any disaster. According to the rules of Greek drama, such events could not be portrayed on stage, and Eliot observes that convention here. Such a parallel serves to remind us, too, that Greek drama was part of a religious festival, and in Eliot's play religious purposes are evident even where disguised by the worldly appearance of such characters as Julia and Alex.

One of the key themes in the play, then, is that of appearance versus reality. The Guardians offer an outstanding example of this theme. It is fitting that it should be Sir Henry Harcourt-Reilly who sums up their identity in his lines in the last Act:

> *For know there are two worlds of life and death:*
> *One that which thou beholdest; but the other*
> *Is underneath the grave, where do inhabit*
> *The shadows of all forms that think and live*
> *Till death unite them and they part no more!*   (p. 174)

The Guardians are at once these 'shadows' and 'that which thou beholdest'.

Part 4

Hints for study

Note-taking

You are preparing for a written examination. This may be a statement of the obvious, but it is useful to bear it in mind. You may be tempted merely to read the text and commentaries on the text. That is, of course, something that is essential. In the end, though, you are going to be tested on your ability to write about the text. The more writing you can do in preparation for your examination, the better. The first kind of writing you will obviously need to undertake is note-taking.

Note-taking techniques vary from one individual to another. Some students are content, for example, to reduce what they know to a few key words on the page. Others are not satisfied until they have crammed all that they know into lists of abbreviated statements. Some like to reproduce facts in columns under significant headings, others prefer a diagrammatic structure in, say, a 'flow-diagram'. There is really no one system that can be said to suit everybody. You must choose the system that suits you best. The only general rule that can be applied is: make notes.

Most notes that you make will be based on your reading of the set text and of commentaries on the set text. When making these notes be sure that they contain careful records of sources. For example, if you choose a quotation from a set text, write down a bracketed note of where you found that statement – it may be an Act or Scene reference, a line reference, or a page reference, or all of these. In making notes on commentaries be sure to make a note of the author of a particular statement, of the title of the book in which it appeared, and of the page in the book where the statement occurs.

Remember, too, to give any series of notes a heading relating to the purpose for which you made those notes.

Planning an essay

The first thing that needs to be said under this heading is that you must always plan your essays, whether in course-work preparation or in your examination. Note that course-work essays need not be planned and written without reference to the text; indeed it is wise to use the text at all times to ensure that your references are accurate.

Planning serves several purposes:

(*a*) it forces you to look at the title of your essay very carefully to examine what is really being asked for;

(*b*) it starts you writing;

(*c*) it helps you to construct your essay methodically;

(*d*) it makes the reading of the essay more attractive to your teacher/ examiner.

The more practice you have in planning essays the simpler the process becomes, so that when you come to sit your examination you will be a practised hand at planning your work, and this will improve your examination performance.

Writing essays

The writing of an essay is as much a skill to the student of literature as the carrying out of an experiment is to a chemistry scholar. The planning of such an essay is comparable to the laboratory practice the chemist must undertake. It ought to be as meticulous and careful and as expert. The chemistry student learns his skill by dint of hours of practice. The literary student has to show the same amount of application. There is no substitute for writing practice. It is not sufficient, for example, merely to read essays provided by others, though a lot can be gained by written analyses of such essays. Thus, you would do well to submit the essay answers provided in this Part (pp. 50–4 below) to such analysis and notes.

The writing of an essay will help to formulate ideas and fix them firmly for you. Your essay notes may look quite workable and well organised. It is only when you come to try to compose an essay based on them that you discover gaps and deficiencies and even redundancies. The writing of an essay helps to give your notes precision and, indeed, validity.

In writing an essay answer be sure that it deals with the question fully. Too often, the examiner's experience is that the candidate deals with only part of a question and omits parts that also demand attention.

What does your examiner expect?

1. Relevance

This is a key word in literature examinations. Candidates have spent some years, say, in academic study of literature. They come to the examination room full of information, and are anxious to divulge as much of it as they can. They feel unduly restricted by the content of the examination question and, in their frustration, wax eloquent and yield to the temptation of irrelevance.

Study is often referred to as 'a discipline' and you ought to bear this word in mind. The student needs to discipline himself to remain relevant. He must stay within the bounds set by the question. In the present instance, for example, the set text is *The Cocktail Party* by T. S. Eliot. Many examinees may wish to demonstrate their acquaintance with details of the author's life. Be careful. Such details, given the nature of questions in literature examinations, may stray into irrelevance. Some candidates may wish to 'impress' the examiner by cross-references to other plays by Eliot. Again, take care. This is a difficult thing to do well and convincingly. The expectation is that you will answer a question set on this text. References to other texts may prove irrelevant.

2. Organisation

The examiner wants to see evidence of planning. It is often useful to demonstrate this planning on the page. Do your plan for the essay, head it PLAN, then draw a line to divide it from your essay proper.

3. Knowledge of text

There is no substitute for this. There must be evidence of first-hand knowledge of the text. Examiners will readily recognise derivative work, second-hand knowledge gleaned from books 'about' the book. References to these are quite acceptable where they are obviously part of your understanding of the text itself.

In poetry and drama texts some quotation is generally welcomed if not expected. Since *The Cocktail Party* is a verse play, quotation is something to make your own. Examples of useful quotations will be found in these Notes in Parts 2, 3 and 4. Quotations from prose works are usually not expected.

4. Cogent argument

This is a quality that is demanded by the nature of questions set on a text such as this. Narrative answers, that is, answers which merely tell the story of the action, will rarely be appropriate. The candidate will be given the opportunity to express a point of view and to argue his case convincingly. He will use skills of organisation and reference. He will employ, too, the skills of fluency and coherence. All of these skills can only be developed through practice. There is then a need to write plenty of essays, and, where the opportunity occurs, of having them assessed.

One function of the specimen answers supplied to questions in this part of these Notes is to provide a point of comparison for the student. You should always attempt such questions yourself first and only then compare your efforts with the suggested answers.

5. Appropriate length

It is difficult to lay down hard-and-fast rules for this. Quality must always take precedence over quantity. Yet there are some considerations of a practical, pragmatic nature. One is that a certain amount of time is allotted to the candidate to write an answer. The time for an examination essay is usually reckoned to be something between forty-five minutes and an hour, though approximations are all that can reasonably be offered here. Given this apportionment of time and the body of material available to the candidate within the context of an examination question, it is not unreasonable to think in terms of an essay of about three pages (sides) in length. Anything much less than that would threaten to be lacking in substance. The candidate could scarcely do himself/herself justice. The maximum length of an examination essay is dictated by the demands of (i) time, (ii) relevance. Make sure always to take both of these factors into account.

Specimen questions and answers

1. How appropriate is it to think of *The Cocktail Party* as a comedy?

PLAN:

Comedy: (1) Method – verbal
                       – characters
                       – stage devices

      (2) Intention – moral purpose
                            – 'comedy of manners'?

ANSWER: It seems eminently appropriate to speak of *The Cocktail Party* as a comedy especially since the author saw it as such. In some editions the title-page of the play boldly claims it to be a comedy.

The opening scene of the play would assure us that the description is accurate. The curtain opens on a bright social scene full of the busy chatter of the guests at a cocktail party. Someone is in the middle of a story and misunderstandings are arising; Julia, for example, asks this inane question of Alex:

Then what were you doing, up in a tree:
You and the Maharaja?

Julia, in her turn, is asked to tell her story about Lady Klootz and the wedding cake. She never tells the story but we are given snippets of it from other characters who have heard it before. Peter Quilpe, for example, provides us with the delightful picture of Lady Klootz rinsing out her mouth with champagne. In its early stages the opening scene consists largely of this kind of light social chit-chat. The tone is trivial but genial. Julia describes it as 'a delightful evening'. The character of Julia is a crucial ingredient in the comedy. This larger-than-life figure is the life and soul of the party. She is an obvious centre of attention and provides a great deal of the fun. So, for example, her teasing of Edward about the absence of Lavinia is a source of amusement to the others. The estrangement between Edward and Lavinia proves to be common knowledge and his vain attempts to explain her absence from the cocktail party readily invite gentle teasing. Julia reduces it to the utterly banal, for example, by saying she is delighted to get Edward away from Lavinia as the only time she had had that opportunity previously was when Lavinia was accidentally locked in the lavatory. Edward's feeble invention of the story that Lavinia had gone to look after a sick aunt is the object of many witty remarks throughout the play.

In addition to the contribution to comedy made by the characterisation of Julia, Eliot uses her to create plenty of movement on stage particularly through unexpected entrances. Having left the cocktail party, for example, she returns twice on trivial pretexts with immediate comic effect. On the first occasion she arrives unannounced to retrieve her umbrella, thus interrupting a serious conversation between Edward and the Unidentified Guest. Julia's intention is blatantly clear: it is to pry. We have already formed the clear impression that she is a gossip and a busybody. Part of the comedy on this occasion is that she attributes these qualities to another guest, Alexander MacColgie Gibbs:

How very lucky it was my umbrella,
And not Alexander's – *he's* so inquisitive!

She interrupts again later in the scene. On this occasion she purports to look for her glasses, and her description of them is amusing in itself. This is a recurring device in this opening scene. It is used again with Alex's return to prepare a meal for Edward. At that point in the scene Edward is involved in a serious conversation with Peter, but this is constantly punctuated by Alex's enquiries about curry powder or a double boiler.

There can be little doubt that the play is a comedy; that was its author's major intention. It has been described as fitting most easily into the literary tradition of a 'comedy of manners', a high form of comedy dealing with exactly the kind of study of society and its domestic troubles which is a feature of *The Cocktail Party*. However, this kind of comedy is still suggestive of the trivial. Eliot's play has a serious moral purpose and, in this, it belongs to another literary tradition which sees comedy as capable of carrying some weight. Much of the rest of the play demonstrates this feature of comedy.

There is still plenty of evidence of the lighter forms of comedy, especially in the verbal exchanges, and in the final act Julia resumes her lively manner. But the purpose has become demonstrably more serious and in keeping with the concept of comedy according to which we laugh at errors in order to avoid falling into them ourselves.

---

2. How far does the following passage summarise the principal ideas in *The Cocktail Party*? Support your answer by reference to the play as a whole.

EDWARD: I see that my life was determined long ago
And that the struggle to escape from it
Is only a make-believe, a pretence
That what is, is not, or could be changed.
The self that can say 'I want this – or want that' –
The self that wills – he is a feeble creature;
He has to come to terms in the end
With the obstinate, the tougher self; who does not speak,
Who never talks, who cannot argue;
And who in some men may be the *guardian*

PLAN:

The self: a new identity needed – a stronger self – of Celia and Peter

Appearance *v.* reality: central theme – exemplified by the cocktail party itself, Edward's lie, Peter's profession

Free will: Reilly's insistence on this – Edward's notion of determinism – need for decision – responsibility for decisions

Sin: not included in Edward's speech here – link between free will and sin – Celia and sin + repentance + atonement

ANSWER: This passage occurs in Edward's conversation with Celia in the second scene of the first act of the play. He has already been counselled by the Unidentified Guest and has given advice to Peter Quilpe. We meet a maturing Edward here, a contrast with the Edward of the early part of the opening scene.

This question of the 'self', of self-identity, is one of the principal ideas in the play and it is central to the passage quoted here. Edward has come to terms with his new self, and it is this self that surprises Celia here. She is forced to confess that Edward is changing for the better:

> I see another person,
> I see you as a person whom I never saw before.
> The man I saw before, he was only a projection –
> I see that now – of something that I wanted

In those lines of Celia's a further idea occurs which is also present in the lines quoted in the given passage. Edward speaks of 'make-believe, a pretence' and Celia speaks of 'a projection'. These various words relate to the conflict in the play between appearances and reality. Eliot is very concerned to show that people place too much stress on external appearances and do not attend to what is real and of true worth. He is especially anxious that we should embrace spiritual reality and scorn the merely material. It is Celia's destiny to be *the* exemplar of abandoning the material for the spiritual. She offers a moral standard for everyone else in the play. Thus Peter, on his return from Hollywood and the world of illusion and, literally, 'projection', comes to recognise the standard that Celia set. He uses it to shape a new approach to life for himself. He will continue to work in the world of films but he will bring a fresh perspective to it. The truth he recognises is:

> That I've only been interested in myself:
> And that isn't good enough for Celia.

This recognition of reality happens at the last cocktail party, quite a different environment to that which Peter found at the first cocktail party which opened the play. There the emphasis was on appearance and appearances, and the reality was ignored. Lavinia's absence, for example, was a reality which Edward was reluctant to face and even more reluctant to betray to others. Instead he hid that reality behind a blatant lie.

Edward is not the most clear-headed of thinkers, and his lie did not carry much weight with his guests. Julia, in particular, created a great deal of comedy by teasing him about Lavinia's whereabouts. In the passage quoted in this question, too, it is obvious that he has not yet clarified in his mind the philosophical position of free will. He offers his rationale for not actively wishing to change the self that he is; it is simply that he feels destined to be what he is, that it has all been 'determined long ago' for him. This is despite the fact that the Unidentified Guest had encouraged him to find out who he really was. The Unidentified Guest, too, had recognised Edward's intellectual deficiencies; he had told him that he was 'nothing but a set/Of obsolete responses' and, even more pointedly: 'Resign yourself to be the fool you are'.

One of the principal ideas in the play is that matters are not 'determined'. Throughout his interviews with the various characters Sir Henry Harcourt-Reilly insists that their way of life has to be their choice. In his dealings with Celia, for example, he says that

> the form of treatment must be your own choice:
> I cannot choose for you.

Once such a decision has been made, however, it must be adhered to. There can be no regression or retraction. As he points out to Edward:

> Your movement of freedom was yesterday.
> You made a decision. You set in motion
> Forces in your life and the lives of others
> Which cannot be reversed.

This last notion, namely that of determinism versus free will, prompts us to refer to an idea which is in the play but on which Edward's words quoted in the question above do not touch. It is the idea of religion. The notion of free will is inherent in the orthodox Christian view of sin. This is a concept that greatly taxes Celia and causes her much anxiety. It may be suggested that since it seems to affect only her it is not a principal concern in the play. However, Celia and her decisions are central to the play and it can thus be reasonably argued that the idea of sin is equally germane. Through Celia, Eliot introduces the notion of Christian morality, of the need for repentance and atonement. It is expressed in a particularly sensational manner in the report of the martyrdom of Celia, crucified like Christ himself. A view of *The Cocktail Party* which omitted this formal religious element would be only a partial view.

Further questions for revision

1. Compare the happenings at the cocktail party in the first scene in the play with those of the second cocktail party in the last act.
2. Discuss the view that Eliot wrote to instruct, not to entertain.
3. Examine the role of Juilia in the play.
4. What features of *The Cocktail Party* would recommend Eliot to you as a dramatist?
5. What features of *The Cocktail Party* did not attract you?
6. '*The Cocktail Party* is a religious play.' Discuss.
7. JULIA: And now, when they are stripped naked to their souls
   And can choose, whether to put on proper costumes
   Or huddle quickly into new disguises,
   They have, for the first time, somewhere to start from.
   (i) To what is Julia referring?
   (ii) How typical of Julia are these lines?
   (iii) What themes in the play can be identified in these lines?
8. You have been asked to write a brief study of *The Cocktail Party* for inclusion in a theatre programme. What features would you choose to highlight for the theatre audience?

Part 5

Suggestions for further reading

The text

ELIOT, T. S.: *The Cocktail Party*, Faber and Faber, London, 1950. (Re-issued in paperback edition, 1958.)

Other works by T. S. Eliot

ELIOT, T. S.: *Selected Essays*, 3rd edition, Faber and Faber, London, 1951. Particular attention should be paid to 'A Dialogue on Dramatic Poetry' (1928), and 'Ben Jonson' (1919).

Criticism

BERGONZI, BERNARD: *T. S. Eliot*, The Macmillan Company, New York, 1972. A comprehensive study of the poet, dramatist and critic, which contains a useful biography.

BRAYBROOK, NEVILLE (ED.): *T. S. Eliot*, Rupert Hart-Davis, London, 1958. This contains a great deal of interesting anecdotal material.

JONES, D. E.: *The Plays of T. S. Eliot*, Routledge and Kegan Paul, London, 1960. This contains a valuable analysis of *The Cocktail Party*.

LUCY, SEAN: *T. S. Eliot and the Idea of Tradition*, Cohen and West, 1960. A difficult book, but well worth tackling.

SMITH, GROVER: *T. S. Eliot's Poetry and Plays: A Study in Sources and Meaning*, 2nd edition, University of Chicago Press, Chicago, 1974. This has some very useful notes on *The Cocktail Party*.

TATE, ALLEN (ED.): *T. S. Eliot, The Man and his Work*, Chatto and Windus, London, 1966. The contributions by Helen Gardner and E. Martin Browne are particularly useful.

WILLIAMS, RAYMOND: *Drama from Ibsen to Eliot*, Chatto and Windus, London, 1952. This offers some useful perspectives on Eliot's contributions to drama.

The author of these notes

DOMINIC HYLAND was educated at St John's College, Cambridge, and at the Universities of Manchester and Lancaster. He teaches with the Open University and Liverpool University Institute of Extension Studies, and is currently Chief Examiner and Moderator in English Language and Literature for one of the largest Examining Boards in the country. He is the author of five York Notes and has produced several revision courses in both Literature and Language.

The first 250 titles

		Series number
THOMAS HARDY (*cont.*)	*Tess of the D'Urbervilles*	(80)
	The Mayor of Casterbridge	(39)
	The Return of the Native	(20)
	The Trumpet Major	(74)
	The Woodlanders	(160)
	Under the Greenwood Tree	(129)
L. P. HARTLEY	*The Go-Between*	(36)
	The Shrimp and the Anemone	(123)
NATHANIEL HAWTHORNE	*The Scarlet Letter*	(134)
ERNEST HEMINGWAY	*A Farewell to Arms*	(145)
	For Whom the Bell Tolls	(95)
	The African Stories	(201)
	The Old Man and the Sea	(11)
GEORGE HERBERT	*Selected Poems*	(233)
HERMANN HESSE	*Steppenwolf*	(135)
BARRY HINES	*Kes*	(189)
ANTHONY HOPE	*The Prisoner of Zenda*	(88)
GERARD MANLEY HOPKINS	*Selected Poems*	(205)
WILLIAM DEAN HOWELLS	*The Rise of Silas Lapham*	(175)
RICHARD HUGHES	*A High Wind in Jamaica*	(17)
THOMAS HUGHES	*Tom Brown's Schooldays*	(2)
ALDOUS HUXLEY	*Brave New World*	(156)
HENRIK IBSEN	*A Doll's House*	(85)
	Ghosts	(131)
	Hedda Gabler	(210)
HENRY JAMES	*Daisy Miller*	(147)
	The Europeans	(120)
	The Portrait of a Lady	(117)
	The Turn of the Screw	(27)
	Washington Square	(234)
SAMUEL JOHNSON	*Rasselas*	(137)
BEN JONSON	*The Alchemist*	(102)
	Volpone	(15)
JAMES JOYCE	*Dubliners*	(250)
JOHN KEATS	*Selected Poems*	(211)
RUDYARD KIPLING	*Kim*	(114)
D. H. LAWRENCE	*Sons and Lovers*	(24)
	The Rainbow	(59)
	Women in Love	(143)
CAMARA LAYE	*L'Enfant Noir*	(191)
HARPER LEE	*To Kill a Mocking-Bird*	(125)
LAURIE LEE	*Cider with Rosie*	(186)
THOMAS MANN	*Tonio Kröger*	(168)
CHRISTOPHER MARLOWE	*Doctor Faustus*	(127)
	Edward II	(166)
ANDREW MARVELL	*Selected Poems*	(235)
W. SOMERSET MAUGHAM	*Of Human Bondage*	(185)
	Selected Short Stories	(38)
J. MEADE FALKNER	*Moonfleet*	(221)
HERMAN MELVILLE	*Billy Budd*	(10)
	Moby Dick	(126)

The first ten titles

YORK HANDBOOKS form a companion series to York Notes and are designed to meet the wider needs of students of English and related fields. Each volume is a compact study of a given subject area, written by an authority with experience in communicating the essential ideas to students of all levels.

AN INTRODUCTORY GUIDE TO ENGLISH LITERATURE
by MARTIN STEPHEN

PREPARING FOR EXAMINATIONS IN ENGLISH LITERATURE
by NEIL McEWAN

AN INTRODUCTION TO LITERARY CRITICISM
by RICHARD DUTTON

THE ENGLISH NOVEL
by IAN MILLIGAN

ENGLISH POETRY
by CLIVE T. PROBYN

STUDYING CHAUCER
by ELISABETH BREWER

STUDYING SHAKESPEARE
by MARTIN STEPHEN *and* PHILIP FRANKS

ENGLISH USAGE
by COLIN G. HEY

A DICTIONARY OF LITERARY TERMS
by MARTIN GRAY

READING THE SCREEN
An Introduction to Film Studies
by JOHN IZOD